812.5 Mer
Merrill, Bob
New girl in town.

T- 28464

Date Due			
4-6-65			

NEW GIRL IN TOWN

New Girl in Town

A NEW MUSICAL

(Based on the play ANNA CHRISTIE, by Eugene O'Neill)

Book by GEORGE ABBOTT
Music and Lyrics by BOB MERRILL

The following songs, including lyrics, were Copyright ©, 1957, by Valyr Music Corporation

FLINGS
IF THAT WAS LOVE
SUNSHINE GIRL
LOOK AT 'ER
AT THE CHECK APRON BALL
DID YOU CLOSE YOUR EYES?
YER MY FRIEND, AINTCHA?
VEN I VALSE
IT'S GOOD TO BE ALIVE
THERE AIN'T NO FLIES ON ME
ANNA LILLA
ROLL YER SOCKS UP
ON THE FARM
CHESS AND CHECKERS

Chappell & Co., Inc., New York, N.Y., sole selling agent for the United States, Canada and Newfoundland. Lyrics used by special permission.

All rights including the right of reproduction in whole or in part, in any form, are reserved under International and Pan-American Copyright Conventions. Published in New York by Random House, Inc., and simultaneously in Toronto, Canada, by Random House of Canada, Limited.

Photographs by courtesy of Friedman-Abeles

Library of Congress Catalog Card Number: 58–6981

MANUFACTURED IN THE
UNITED STATES OF AMERICA

NEW GIRL IN TOWN *was first presented by Frederick Brisson, Robert E. Griffith and Harold S. Prince at the Forty-Sixth Street Theatre, New York City, on May 14, 1957, with the following cast:*

(AS THEY APPEAR)

LILY	Lulu Bates
MOLL	Pat Ferrier
KATIE	Mara Lynn
ALDERMAN	Michael Quinn
CHRIS	Cameron Prud'homme
JOHNSON	Jeff Killion
OSCAR	Del Anderson
SEAMAN (First Mate)	H. F. Green
MARTHY	Thelma Ritter
MRS. SMITH	Dorothy Stinnette
PETE	Eddie Phillips
IVY	Rita Noble
ROSE	Ginny Perlowin
BARTENDER (Larry)	Mark Dawson
ANNA	Gwen Verdon
PEARL	Mara Landi
FLO	Drusilla Davis
SVENSON	Ray Mason
MAT	George Wallace
MRS. DOWLING	Ann Williams
REPORTER	Herb Fields
SMITH	Stokley Gray
MASHER	John Aristides
WAITER	Louis Polacek
MRS. HAMMACHER	Jean Handzlik
DOWLING	Ripple Lewis
POLITICIAN	H. F. Green

KRIMP	John Ford
HENRY	Edgar Daniels
VIOLET	Deedy Irwin

DANCERS: Claiborne Cary, Drusilla Davis, Dorothy Dushock, Pat Ferrier, Marie Kolin, Mara Lynn, Ethel Martin, Joan Petlak, John Aristides, Robert Bakanic, Harvey Hohnecker, Harvey Jung, Dale Moreda, John Nola, Eddie Phillips, Alton Ruff.

SINGERS: Jean Handzlik, Deedy Irwin, Mara Landi, Rita Noble, Ginny Perlowin, Dorothy Stinnette, Ann Williams, Del Anderson, Edgar Daniels, Herb Fields, John Ford, Stokley Gray, H. F. Green, Jeff Killion, Ripple Lewis, Ray Mason, Louis Polacek, Michael Quinn.

Production directed by George Abbott
Dances and musical numbers staged by Bob Fosse
Production designed by Rouben Ter-Arutunian
Musical direction by Hal Hastings
Orchestrations by Robert Russell Bennett and Philip J. Lang
Dance music devised by Roger Adams

MUSICAL NUMBERS

ACT ONE

ROLL YER SOCKS UP	H. F. Green, Dancers and Singers
ANNA LILLA	Cameron Prud'homme
SUNSHINE GIRL	Del Anderson, Eddie Phillips and Mark Dawson
ON THE FARM	Gwen Verdon
FLINGS	Thelma Ritter, Lulu Bates and Mara Landi
IT'S GOOD TO BE ALIVE	Gwen Verdon
LOOK AT 'ER	George Wallace
IT'S GOOD TO BE ALIVE (Reprise)	George Wallace
YER MY FRIEND, AINTCHA?	Thelma Ritter and Cameron Prud'homme
DID YOU CLOSE YOUR EYES?	Gwen Verdon and George Wallace
AT THE CHECK APRON BALL	Dancers and Singers
THERE AIN'T NO FLIES ON ME	Gwen Verdon and Company

ACT TWO

VEN I VALSE	Gwen Verdon, Cameron Prud'homme, Dancers and Singers
SUNSHINE GIRL (Reprise)	Dancers and Singers
IF THAT WAS LOVE	Gwen Verdon
BALLET	Gwen Verdon, John Aristides, and Dancers
CHESS AND CHECKERS	Thelma Ritter, Dancers and Singers
LOOK AT 'ER (Reprise)	George Wallace

The action takes place in New York City, on the waterfront, shortly after the turn of the century.

ACT ONE

ACT ONE

SCENE 1

THE WATERFRONT. *A dock with ships in the background and buildings at either side. There is a shack, over the door of which is written "Office." On the side of this building is written "Atlantic Coal Company." There are various people walking around—some prostitutes and some wives waiting for men, and sailors who from time to time go into the office to get their pay.*

LILY

(An aging trollop)
I tell you, this place is a gold mine.

MOLL

Where are they all?

LILY

But I always claim it's the best spot on the waterfront.
(ALDERMAN *enters with greenhorn sailor.*)

ALDERMAN

. . . And you can become a member of the Young People's Democratic Club.

KATIE

Stick to sailors.

MOLL

But where are they?

3

LILY

There's a ship comin' in this mornin'. They'll be here.

KATIE

Hey, here comes a sailor.

LILY

No, that's old Chris. He's got a woman. Hello, Chris.
(CHRIS CHRISTOPHERSON *enters. He is a jovial weather-beaten sea captain. At this moment he stumbles somewhat unsteadily on his feet.*)

CHRIS

Hey, Lily. Hello, Yonson.

JOHNSON
(*One of the sailors*)
Say, Captain, Marthy was lookin' for you.

CHRIS

I don't want to see Marthy. I don't want to go home for long time yet.
(GIRLS *sing*)
Roll yer socks up, fling 'em in your gearbox.
(CHRIS *staggers*.)

JOHNSON

Easy, Captain.

MOLL

He's a captain?

LILY

Of a coal barge. Bah.

ALDERMAN

(*To another sailor standing around*)
And you, too, my fine friend. The Check Apron Ball. Greatest
social event of the season.

OSCAR

Oh, sure, I heard about that one.
(*Offstage cheering of sailors.*)

MOLL

Here comes some of them.

KATIE

They're gonna get paid, huh?

LILY

Yeah, but don't get so anxious. You've got to give them a
little come on. Hey, Chris, you want to buy me a drink?

CHRIS

Sure, I buy you drink. I buy everybody drink.
(*Sailors enter carrying gear. Prostitutes tag along.*)

FIRST SAILOR

Home, sweet home.

FIRST GIRL

Hello, big boy.

SECOND SAILOR

Look at those babes.

MOLL

Look at me.

THIRD SAILOR

Pay money, here I come.

SECOND GIRL

He's for me.

FOURTH SAILOR

Hello, peachy.

THIRD GIRL

Don't worry, I'll wait.

FIFTH SAILOR

Look at 'em, will ya, just look at 'em.

OSCAR

Here she comes.

(FIRST MATE *sings*)
Roll yer socks up,
Fling 'em in yer gearbox.

(SEAMAN)
Roll yer socks up,
Fling 'em in yer gearbox.
Shave yer face up,
Smell like a violet.
Okev doke, jack,

Blow it out the smokestack.
Tell Creation we're home.
Roll, ship, roll homeward
Roll, ship, roll
Roll, we're home.

(GIRLS)
Roll yer socks up,
Fling 'em in yer gearbox.
Shave yer face up,
Smell like a violet.
Okey doke, jack,
Blow it out the smokestack.
Tell Creation we're home.

(FIRST MATE)
We got some awful big ideas

(SEAMAN)
Awful big ideas

(FIRST MATE)
We should hush, not tell ya.

(SEAMAN)
We should shush, not tell ya.
'Cause you'll blush if we tell ya
our ideas.

(GIRLS)
First a lecture at da Academy,

(SEAMAN)
Den a trip to da public library,

(GIRLS)
Da aquarium is fun we hear.

(CHRIS)
Don't anybody vant a beer?

(SEAMAN)
Gonna read a book 'cause it's such a thrill,

(GIRLS)
Gonna pick some flowers on da hill,

(SEAMAN)
Den off to da park to feed a squirrel.

(GIRLS)
Don't anybody want a girl?
A girl, a girl,
Don't anybody want a girl?
    (*They go into a rowdy dance*)
Roll yer socks up
Fling 'em in yer gearbox.
Shave yer face up,
Smell like a violet,
Okey doke, jack,
Blow it out the smokestack.
Tell Creation we're a-comin' home,
We're a-comin' home, we're a-comin' home,
    we're home.
    (*At the end of the number* MARTHY *enters—a bedraggled
    harridan wearing an oversized man's sweater and men's
    shoes.*)

JOHNSON

Here comes Marthy.

CHRIS

Come on, now, have fun with me. (Sees MARTHY) Oh, oh, I
don't play no more. Here's friend of mine.

MARTHY

You old fool.

CHRIS

Now, Marthy.

MARTHY

What are you tryin' to do, ditch me?

CHRIS

No, I—

MARTHY

Gettin' drunk all by yourself. Ain't that selfish of you. Well,
you took the wrong time for it. I'll tell you that, squarehead;
this time I had important news for you. And I got a notion not
to tell you.

CHRIS

I vas lookin' all around for you.

MARTHY

Ah, quit yer lyin', Dutchy. I know you and you know me.

CHRIS

Ay yust have vun liddle drink.

MARTHY

Vun liddle drink. You gotta breath like the Jersey flats.

CHRIS

Ve have bad trip, Marthy; damn fog come down. Py golly, ven ve get shore ve need drink.

MARTHY

Very sad, very sad, but you always need vun liddle drink.

CHRIS

You lookin' pretty nice today, Marthy.
(*He tries to put his arms around her.*)

MARTHY

(*Pulling away*)
Leave me be—you terrible disgustin' creature.

CHRIS

It's all right, Marthy, I got some money left.

MARTHY

Oh, here.
(*She passes an envelope to him.*)

CHRIS

Vat is it?

MARTHY

It come yesterday. It was sent to Larry's saloon. And when I seen the name on the outside, I opened it.

CHRIS

(*Looks at the envelope*)

From my Anna.

MARTHY

She's comin' to see you.

CHRIS

Vat you say, Marthy?

MARTHY

A fine drunken father she's goin' to find when she gets here.

CHRIS

Anna. Ven she come?

MARTHY

Right now, for all I know. She left St. Paul two days ago.

CHRIS

I gotta sober up. Vere ve goin' find her?

MARTHY

At Larry's saloon, I told you. That's the only address you give her.

CHRIS

Ay can't tank good, Marthy. You come. You help me.

MARTHY

Sure.

CHRIS

Anna. Vy she comin'? I don't know vat to do now. Oh, Marthy—

MARTHY

Come on, I'll help.

(*She leads him offstage. More sailors enter singing "Roll Yer Socks Up" and streetwalkers jeer at them.*)

A street. A mesh fence separates it from the water's edge. Two proper women, carrying groceries, cross the stage.

MRS. SMITH

. . . Well, we're planning to move to a better neighborhood. (MARTHY *and* CHRIS *enter, as the women continue walking to the end of the street and exit.*)

MARTHY

A nurse—that what she is? A nurse?

CHRIS

Dat's vat her letter say—must be year ago. Now she come find ole fool fadder drunk.

MARTHY

I've seen you worse. At least you're on your feet. Listen, Dutchy, I'll meet the kid. You go over to McCloskey's saloon and get sobered up. If she's on that four o'clock train like she says, she might be there right now. You don't want her hangin' around no barroom, do you?

CHRIS

No, Marthy, no.
(CHRIS *sings*)
Da last time Ay see Anna, she tiny like a pea.
In all my life Ay don't forget how vunce she say to me;
"Ay love you, Pa, Ay love you, Pa," dis peewee say to me.

13

(*Speaks*)
Anna Lilla. Ay don't see Anna since she vas liddle gel in Sveden, five year old.

MARTHY

I thought you told me Minnesota.

CHRIS

Ven her mudder die, Anna go live vid cousins in Minnesota. Now she come find ole fool fadder drunk. My poor liddle gel.

MARTHY

Sure, Dutchy, you ain't hardly mentioned her for fifteen years.

CHRIS

But Ay love my Anna yust the same—Ay tank about her— Ay don't say nodding, but Ay tank.

MARTHY

Well, Ay tank you better go put your head under a faucet and drink some black coffee. I'll be over to Larry's havin' a beer.
(*She exits.*)

(CHRIS *sings to the crumpled letter*)
Anna Lilla, Anna Lilla, Anna Lilla mine,
Alvays in my heart you shine.
You vant your pa—You vant your pa,
Like good gel should, you love your pa.
Anna, your papa loves you.

Anna Lilla, Anna Lilla, Anna Lilla mine,
Could you maybe say, "Pa, Ay vant to stay"?
Anna mine.

    (CHRIS *exits.*)

SCENE 3

Johnny-the-Priest's saloon, divided into two sections: the ladies' section on the right, with two tables; the bar on the left.

Two streetwalkers are seated at a table in the ladies' section. LARRY, *the bartender, is behind the bar, reading a newspaper.* PETE *and* OSCAR, *two jovial drunks, are standing at the bar singing snatches of a ragtime tune.*

> (PETE *sings*)

He gave her kisses 'n promised the moon.

ROSE

Here's luck.

IVY

Down she goes.
> (*The streetwalkers exit.*)

> (PETE, *still singing*)

But now he's singin' a different tune.
> (*Speaks*)

That's the song for me.

LARRY

Sure, it's the latest thing. Straight from the Great White Way. (*Puts beer on bar*) Here you are.

OSCAR

Play it again, will you, Pete?

16

PETE

Sure thing. (*Walks up towards player piano, singing "He left her waitin' alone at the church," meanwhile looking for money. Stops*) Give me a nickel, pal.

OSCAR

(*Searching for change*)

It's the kind of song that makes you feel good. (*Gives nickel to* PETE) That's the way I am, Larry, I like a song that makes me feel good.

(PETE *puts nickel in player piano, turns and kicks it sharply with the heel of his shoe. The honky-tonk tune strikes up, and he makes his way back to the bar.*)

(LARRY)

He gave her kisses 'n promised the moon,
But now he's singin' a different tune.

(OSCAR)

He left her waitin' alone at the church,
He left her waitin' alone in the lurch.

(ALL THREE)

With all her broken dreams it's no surprise
The Sunshine Girl has raindrops in her eyes.

(*Buzzer sounds.* LARRY *goes to the ladies' entrance and lets in a* LITTLE GIRL *in pigtails who is rushing the growler.*)

(OSCAR *and* PETE)

You hear them fallin' a-pitter 'n pat,
She wears a rain cloud instead of a hat,
She still remembers the day that they met,

She may forgive him but never forget.
> (LARRY *returns to the bar carrying the empty can, which*
> *he fills with beer and returns to the child.*)

(ALL THREE)
An angel's heart became the devil's prize,
The Sunshine Girl has raindrops in her eyes,
The Sunshine Girl has raindrops in her eyes.
> (PETE *does a good-natured goofy dance.*)

(OSCAR *and* PETE)
You hear them fallin' a-pitter 'n pat,
She wears a rain cloud instead of a hat,
She still remembers the day that they met,
She may forgive him but never forget.

(ALL THREE)
An angel's heart became the devil's prize,
The Sunshine Girl has raindrops in her eyes,
The Sunshine Girl has raindrops in her eyes.
> (MARTHY *comes to the ladies' entrance.*)

MARTHY

It's me again.

LARRY

(*Admitting her*)
Couldn't you find old Chris?

MARTHY

He'll be here. There ain't been a little girl lookin' for him,
was there?

LARRY

A little girl?

MARTHY

Well, a big girl maybe. Kind of like a nurse.

LARRY

We could use a good nurse around here, but I ain't seen one today. What'll it be?

MARTHY

Bring me a schooner.

LARRY

Schooner.
(*He returns to the bar.*)

OSCAR

Come on, Larry, have one with us.

LARRY

I don't drink, boys. I'll have a cigar.

PETE

To hell with it. Let's go down the line.

OSCAR

No, let's have a drink first.

PETE

We already had a drink.

OSCAR

Oh, I forgot.
(*They exit, singing.*)
He gave her kisses 'n promised the moon,
But—now he's singin' a different tune—
(LARRY *brings the beer to* MARTHY, *putting it down a little carelessly, and it slops over her.*)

MARTHY

Look what you're doin', you fat slob.

LARRY

(*Wiping table*)
Spoil your party dress, Marthy?

MARTHY

Aw, get out of here.
(*The buzzer sounds. He goes to the door and opens it.* ANNA CHRISTOPHERSON *enters. Still young but beaten, she is dressed garishly. She comes wearily into the room, and sinks onto a bench at the other table.*)

ANNA

Gimme a whiskey—ginger ale on the side. (*Then, as* LARRY *turns to go, forcing a winning smile at him*) And don't be stingy, baby.

LARRY

(*Sarcastically*)
Shall I serve it in a pail?

ANNA

(*With a hard laugh*)

That suits me down to the ground. (LARRY *goes into the bar.* THE TWO WOMEN *size each other up with frank stares.* LARRY *comes back with a drink which he sets before* ANNA, *and returns to the bar again.* ANNA *downs her drink at a gulp. Then, after a moment, as the alcohol begins to rouse her, she turns to* MARTHY *with a friendly smile*) Boy, I needed that bad, all right, all right!

MARTHY

Sure—you look all in. Been on a bat?

ANNA

No—traveling—day and a half on the train. Had to sit up all night in the dirty coach, too. Gawd, I thought I'd never get here.

MARTHY

(*With a start—looking at her intently*)

Where'd you come from, huh?

ANNA

St. Paul—out in Minnesota.

MARTHY

(*Staring at her slowly*)

Oh—ho, ho—oh.

(*She suddenly bursts out into hoarse, ironical laughter.*)

ANNA

What you laughin' at? Me?

MARTHY

(*Stops laughing*)

Not you.

ANNA

Guess I do look rotten—just out of the hospital two weeks. I'm goin' to have another. What d'you say?

MARTHY

Sure I will. Thanks. (*She calls*) Hey, Larry! Little service!

ANNA

I gotta meet someone. (LARRY *comes in*) Same for me.

MARTHY

Same here.
(LARRY *takes the glasses and goes.*)

ANNA

Well, there ain't anythin' wrong with me, is there? You're sure lookin' hard enough.

MARTHY

Don't have to look much. I got your number the minute you set foot in that door.

ANNA

I got yours, too. You're me forty years from now.

MARTHY

Is that so? Well, anyways, I didn't just get out of no hospital.

ANNA

Ain't you the wisenheimer! (*Shrugs*) Ain't nothin' like that. Thanks just as much.

(LARRY *brings the drinks.* ANNA *pays.*)

MARTHY

I'm just pullin' your leg. Here's to you. (*Raises glass.* ANNA *sulks*) No hard feelin's, huh?

ANNA

Sure. You're right. Skoal.

MARTHY

Mud in your eye.

(MARTHY *drinks half her beer.*)

ANNA

(*Suddenly begins to talk*)

The joint I was in out in St. Paul got raided. Thirty days the judge give us. Some of them didn't mind, but it got my goat. I couldn't sleep or eat or nothin'. So they sent me to a hospital. (*Finishes her drink*) Come on, let's have another one.

MARTHY

You better go easy—hadn't you? Didn't you say you was goin' to meet someone?

ANNA

Yes. Oh, not what you think. It's my old man I got to meet. He might be willin' to stake me to a room and eats till I get rested up. (*Resignedly*) But I ain't countin' on it. Give you a kick when you're down, that's what all men do. (*With sudden passion*) And I don't expect he'll turn out no better than the rest.

MARTHY

This one'll turn out real good.

ANNA

Oh, sure.

MARTHY

It's old Chris, ain't it?

ANNA

Old Chris?

MARTHY

Chris Christopherson.

ANNA

How'd you know?

MARTHY

I took him your letter, that's how. He sent me over here to keep track of you.

ANNA

Honest?

MARTHY

He thinks you're a nurse.

ANNA

Well, sure, I had to write him somethin'. What's he like?

MARTHY

Oh, he's a big feller—

ANNA

(*Impatiently*)

I don't care what he looks like. What kind is he?

MARTHY

He's as good-hearted as they come. So quit worrying. He'll give you his shirt—and probably mine too. He's so glad you're comin' that he's cryin'.

ANNA

Cryin'?

MARTHY

Sure. He ain't forgot you. He told me all about you. How he kept you in the country where you'd be safe.

ANNA

Where he wouldn't have to bother with me, you mean. Where they treat you worse than a hired girl. Them nephews. That's when I got started, when I was sixteen. Then every one of them was after me. I ran away. More men. So I ended up in a house. I hate them, every mother's son of them. I hate them.

(CHRIS *enters the men's bar, coming cautiously, now cleaned up and sober.*)

CHRIS

Py golly, Larry—

MARTHY

Sh!

CHRIS

Somebody come for me?

ANNA

What's up?

LARRY

Marthy's in there. Some other tramp with her.

MARTHY

That's him. He's comin' in. Brace up.

ANNA

My father.

MARTHY

(*Goes to door leading to the bar—calls*)
Well, hello, old Chris. I got somethin' for you in here. (MAR-THY *goes to the street door*) So long, kid, I'm going to beat it. See you later.
(*She exits.* CHRIS *comes over to the ladies' side as* LARRY *resumes reading his paper. He hesitates a second, walks in and looks at* ANNA. *To him, her finery is beautiful.*)

CHRIS

Anna.

ANNA

Hello, Father. She told me it was you. I just got here a little while ago.

CHRIS

(*Goes slowly over to her chair*)
It's good—for see you—after all dem years, Anna.

ANNA

It's good to see you, too.

CHRIS

(*Grasps her arms and looks into her face—then, overcome by a wave of fierce tenderness*)
Anna Lilla! Anna Lilla!

ANNA

(*Shrinks away from him, half-frightened*)
What's that—Swedish? I don't know it. (*Then, as if seeking relief from the tension in a voluble chatter*) Gee, I had an awful trip comin' here. I'm all in. And then I had a hard job findin' this place. I never been in New York before, you know.

CHRIS

Ay'm glad you here, Anna.

ANNA

Sure. Why didn't you never come to see me?

CHRIS

Ay make plan to come. One time Ay'm all ready for start, den some fellow pick my pocket—lost ticket—everyting.

ANNA

Tough luck.

CHRIS

But Ay know you have nice home in Minnesota.

27

ANNA

Oh, sure, dandy.

CHRIS

Ay always know you have good life on farm.

ANNA

You bet. I'll tell you about it some time.
> (*She sings to him. He looks at her adoringly, only half-hearing her words*)

See my rosy cheeks, my sunny disposish,
Ya can see I grew up fine as silk,
Ya put me on the farm, far away from harm,
All kids need to grow up nice is milk.

On the farm, on the farm, far away from any harm,
Country butter, eggs by the dozens,
Gettin' grabbed by all the cousins,
On the farm, on the farm.

Pretty birds, pretty brooks, like ya see in picture books,
In the barn with Uncle Jake,
If ya squeal, ya get the rake,
On the farm, on the farm.

Uncle Sven was kind of a preacher,
Would have made a swell school teacher,
Studied all the natch-ral habits
Of the horses, cows 'n rabbits,
I was teacher's pet,
I learned some things I'll never forget.

On the farm, on the farm, far away from any harm,
Lots of bees all makin' honey,

Lots of sun makes people sunny,
On the farm, on the farm.

Mary was a little lamb, till everybody caught 'er,
Mary took it on the lam, 'cause lambs get led to slaughter.
On the farm, on the farm, any girl is safe from harm,
Might have grown up in the city,
Never knowin' it's so pretty,
On the farm, on the farm,
With those vicious sons of bitches on the farm.
    (ANNA *speaks*)
I need a drink.

CHRIS

Vat, Anna?

ANNA

Oh, nothin'. I was just sort of thirsty.

CHRIS

Ay'm sorry, Anna. Vat you tank you like for drink, eh?

ANNA

I'll take a—(*Then suddenly reminded—confusedly*) I don't
know. What'a they got here?

CHRIS
(*With a grin*)

Ay don't tank dey got much fancy drink for a young gal in dis
place, Anna. Yinger Ale—sas-prilla, maybe.

ANNA

Make it sas, then.

29

CHRIS

(*Coming up to her—with a wink*)

Ay tell you, Anna, ve celebrate, yes—dis vun time, because ve meet after many year. (*In a half-whisper, embarrassedly*) Dey got good port vine, Anna. Vun glass don't go to your head, Ay promise.

ANNA

(*With a half-hysterical laugh*)

All right. I'll take port.

CHRIS

Ay go gat him.
(*He goes to the bar.* ANNA *sits and lets her head fall on her arms.*)

LARRY

(*Putting down his paper as* CHRIS *comes toward him—with a grin*)

Well, who's the blonde?

CHRIS

(*Proudly*)

Dat vas Anna, Larry.

LARRY

(*In amazement*)

Your daughter Anna?
(CHRIS *nods.*)

CHRIS

Give me a drink for to take back. Vun port vine for Anna. Don't you tank she vas pooty gel, Larry?

30

LARRY

Sure! A peach!

CHRIS

You bet you! She celebrate dis vun time vid me—and small beer for me.

LARRY

Small beer, eh? She's reformin' you already.

CHRIS

(*Pleased*)

You bet! (*He takes the drinks. As she hears him coming,* ANNA *hastily dries her eyes, tries to smile.* CHRIS *comes in and sets the drinks down on the table*) Listen, Anna, Ay got little place here vere you can stay for a couple of days. Den ve go on barge for trip to Boston. Tugs come and tow us out. Vater all around, sun, fresh air, good grub make you strong, healthy girl.

ANNA

Sounds good, little trip on the water.

CHRIS

You bet she ban good. (*Raises glass. She lifts her glass. He grins*) Skoal, Anna! You know dat Svedish vord?

ANNA

Skoal. Guess I know that word, all right.
(ANNA *downs the port at a gulp, as though it were a drink of whiskey;* CHRIS *drinks slowly.*)

31

SCENE 4

A street in the warehouse district, stacked high with crates. A child is skipping rope. There is considerable traffic of people. MARTHY *and* CHRIS *enter through a gate.*

MARTHY

Sure, sure, you're an ideal father. Tell me more, Dutchy. Where is she? What are you doin' here?

CHRIS

She vait down at barge.

MARTHY

What you got her there for? Ain't it more comfortable in our little old flat?

CHRIS

(*Apologetic*)

Marthy—innocent young gel like dat? How could Ay? If she see you dere, vat she tank?

MARTHY

Oh, I can see what's comin'. I can see what's in the back of your nut. Get rid of me, huh? The bum's rush for old Marthy.

32

CHRIS

All my life, Ay never treat my Anna good. Ay got to make up now. Ay got to do good by her.

MARTHY

I can see it comin' a mile off. Ho, ho, you're a scream. Well, listen, don't start nothin'.

CHRIS

Ay don't start nodding.

MARTHY

Who asked me to move in there? And now, outscray. Call the bouncer. Throw her to the dogs. No, you can't get away with that. (*Some neighbors, attracted by the commotion, drift in.* MARTHY *turns to* LILY *and* PEARL, *a pair of tarnished old jaybirds*) You should hear the squarehead.

CHRIS

(*Desperately*)

Listen, Marthy, Vednesday ve go to Boston on barge, den you move back.

MARTHY

Send me a note. I'll be havin' tea with the Rockefellers. Oh, how I hate the changeability of people. First I get used to you as a drunken friend and now I gotta start all over again and get used to you as a father.

CHRIS

No, Marthy, Ay still be drunken friend.

33

MARTHY

Get out—get out!
>(*She hits and even kicks him offstage.* FLO *and* MOLL, *of
>the younger streetwalking set, cackle.*)

FLO and MOLL

Give it to him—give it to him. Kick him in the pants.

MARTHY

(*Comes back*)
Tells me I gotta get out 'cause his daughter is here. I ain't good
enough.

MOLL

Don't stand for it.

FLO

Give him the gate, Marthy.

MARTHY

Hell of a friend he turned out to be.

LILY

He'll be back.

MOLL

If it happened to me I'd fix him plenty.

FLO

Sure, have yourself a fling.

34

MARTHY

Me?

LILY

Aw, go chase yourselves. You fly-by-night kids don't know what's good for a girl like Marthy.

PEARL

She don't pay them no attention.

LILY

Wait'll they've had experience. Flings.
(*Sings*)
Flings. Flings is wonderful things,

(MARTHY)
And they got to be flung,
But some day when your springs are sprung;

(PEARL)
Then it's nice to have someone to yak with,

(LILY)
Sit around with; scratch a back with.

(MARTHY)
Any hand which buys your sandwich,
You can love.

(PEARL)
Flings. Flings is wonderful things,
When you're young you can whoop,

(LILY)
But some day when your feathers droop,

(MARTHY)
Then it's nice to have a bird to chirp with,
Have a beer with, have a burp with.

(ALL THREE)
Though it's quiet, when you try it, gee, it's nice.

(LILY)
When some Romeo would twinkle,
Why, my skin just used to pinkle,

(MARTHY)
Now just bring me Rip Van Winkle and it's love.

(PEARL)
What they say is the truth,
There ain't nothin' like youth,

(LILY)
When you're right at your peak,
But some day when your hinges creak,

(PEARL)
If there's fire in a guy he'll lose it,

(MARTHY)
If he had it, who could use it?

(LILY)
So you sit there countin' pains and saving string,

(ALL THREE)
And rememberin' flings, flings is wonderful things,
But they got to be flung by the young.

(MARTHY)
Flings, flings is wonderful things,

(PEARL)
When the battle is hot,

(MARTHY)
But some day when your shells are shot,

(PEARL)
You don't want a guy who's all inspired,

(MARTHY)
Please believe me, you'll get tired,

(LILY)
Let him snooze off with his shoes off,
It's all right.

(PEARL)
As a girl I'd start in seethin'
Over guys just finished teethin',

(MARTHY)
Now if they're alive and breathin'
That's enough.

(LILY)
At a hundred and nine
Any girl can do fine
If she'll only resign
That she isn't sweet Adeline,

(PEARL)
'Cause a guy don't need a gal
To thrill 'im

(MARTHY)
If she'd thrill 'im it might kill 'im,

(ALL THREE)
So you sit there
While the damn canary sings,
And remember your flings.
Flings is wonderful things,
But they got to be flung
By the young.

Scene 5

CHRIS's *barge, on a foggy night at sea, off Provincetown. In the foreground is the barge with the coil of rope downstage and the cabin right, a dim light showing through its window. In the background is the sea; and far away a passing ship makes a light which rises and falls gently on the horizon. There is the sound of the waves washing against the barge, as if pulled through the water, and the sound of the wind. A tug which is pulling the barge is offstage, left, and we hear, on occasion, its warning signal as it plows through the fog.* ANNA *sits looking out at the sea. She wears a black coat. She looks healthy and transformed. The door to the cabin opens and* CHRIS *sticks his head out. He is blinded by the change in light.*

CHRIS

Anna! (*Receiving no reply, he calls again, this time with apparent apprehension*) Anna!

ANNA

Yes, here I am. What d'you want?

CHRIS

(*Walks over to her*)
It ain't good for you stay out here in fog, Ay tank.

39

ANNA

Why not? (*With a trace of strange exultation*) I love this fog.
Honest, It's so—(*She hesitates, groping for a word*) Funny and
still. I feel as if I was—out of things altogether.

CHRIS

Ay'm glad you like it on barge. Ay'm glad it makes you feel
good again. (*With a placating grin*) You like live like dis alone
with ole fadder, eh?

ANNA

Sure I do. Everythin's been so different from anythin' I ever
come across. All the way to Boston the sun shinin', and now—
this fog—Gee, I wouldn't have missed it for nothin'.

CHRIS

You act funny tonight, Anna.

ANNA

(*Sharply*)
What's funny about it? You want me to like it and I like it.
Aw, come on, sit down for a while.
(CHRIS *sits down with a sigh.*)

CHRIS

Getting pooty late. Must be near five bells.

ANNA

I sure like that sea talk. If I was you I'd be sailing on a real
ship all around the world.

CHRIS

Ay sail many long year, Anna, ven Ay vas damn fool. On coast of Sveden all men vas sailors. My fadder die on four-mast barque two days from Sydney. Two brodder go down in North Sea. But me, py golly, Ay bet you Ay die ashore in bed.

ANNA

So they was all sailors. I like that.

CHRIS

Sailors no good.

ANNA

I don't care. If I was a man I'd be a sailor. I feel right at home out here. I feel all cleaned up, all new, inside and out.
(*There is a staccato blast from the tug.*)

CHRIS

Vell—now vat dey vant? (*To* ANNA) Ay go see vat's goin' on, almanac—dat put you to sleep.
Ay be back. You better turn in, Anna. Read coal company

ANNA

I ain't sleepy.
(CHRIS *exits.* ANNA *moves to the edge of the ship, leans over the side, running her hand dreamily in the water. She sings*)
The brightest paper Valentine,
Has nothin' on this heart of mine,
In spite of me, it's singin', "Gee,
It's good to be alive!"

41

I figgered me a hopeless case,
I thought a smile would break my face,
But all along I figgered wrong,
It's good to be alive!

Just like a clock, I'd tick and tock,
And nothin' was a kick,
But now I'm glad I'm livin',
'Cause I know what makes me tick.

Life never seemed so sweet before,
Like all the world's a candy store,
And tho' it's been there all the time,
I'm like a kid who found a dime,
It's all for me,
It's good to be alive.

(*At the end of her song, there is the sound of a commotion coming from the tug.* JOHNSON, *a crew member, runs on excitedly, crosses to the cabin.*)

JOHNSON

Aye, aye, sir.

SVENSON
(*Off-stage*)

Get a hold of him.

MAT
(*Off-stage*)

I'm all right.

SVENSON
(*Off-stage*)

Get a hold of him, I told you.

42

ANNA

What's the matter?

JOHNSON

They're pickin' up a boat. She's alongside up forward.
(*He runs and opens the cabin door.* CHRIS *hurries on.*)

SVENSON
(*Off-stage*)

I'll take this one.

MAT
(*Off-stage*)

I'll take myself.

CHRIS

Anna, you get vhiskey in cabin qvick.

ANNA

What is it? What happened?

CHRIS

Sailors fellas. Get some blankets.
(*More commotion and voices are heard off-stage.*)

ANNA
(*Starting toward cabin*)

Where'd they come from?

CHRIS

Dey ban two days in open boat. Steamer got wrecked.

MAT
(*Off-stage*)

I'm all right. Look after them two.

CHRIS

Vun fella still on his feet. Other two pooty far gone. (CHRIS *helps bring two collapsed sailors into the cabin.* ANNA *goes in with them*) Ve fix you boys up. Vere's da big vun?

JOHNSON

He's comin'. Wouldn't let me help him. Said he could walk.

CHRIS

Come on, inside with him, Yonson.

JOHNSON

We put him in the bunk.
    (*They exit into the cabin. Then* MAT BURKE *enters. A big bruiser, he wears only dungaree pants, walks unsteadily toward the cabin.*)

MAT

I don't need no help, I can walk. (*Stops and begins to laugh— thumps his chest with his fists exultantly*) Ho, ho, I ain't dead. *The door opens and* ANNA *steps out with a glass of whiskey in her hand. They are startled to see each other. He turns his head and shakes it like a boxer. Then he looks back*) Maybe I am dead.

ANNA

(*Offering the glass*)

Here, drink this.

MAT

It's a woman. A real live woman.

44

ANNA

Go on—drink. You need it, I guess.

MAT

Or am I dreamin'?

ANNA

What a nut— Do you want it or don't you? Here.
(MAT *takes the glass.*)

MAT

Whatever you say. (*Drinks. Shakes off effect*) Wow! You're
still here.

ANNA

In there they got a place for you to lie down.

MAT

I like it here.
(*He grabs her.*)

ANNA

(*Jerking away—she knocks the glass out of his hand*)
Cut it out.

MAT

How about a kiss for a dyin' sailor? You know what I thought
at first—I thought you was a mermaid.

ANNA

Well, I'm not. So get in there.

MAT

To hell with it, I like it out here.

45

ANNA

And I don't care for your language. The men I know don't pull that kind of rough stuff around ladies.

MAT

Have a heart, baby. I've been at sea for four months. I've had a ship sunk under me. I thought I had seen my last woman, and here I am standin' safe—close enough to touch you.

ANNA

Well, don't try it.

MAT

Why not?

ANNA

Because—

MAT

What'll you do?

ANNA

Well, for one thing, I'll yell. And my father will come out here and crack your thick skull with a belayin' pin.

MAT

(*Taken aback*)

Your father?

ANNA

So just wait till day after tomorrow when we get to New York and there'll be plenty of what you're lookin' for all over the waterfront.

(MAT *sits down, stunned.*)

46

MAT

(*Thumping his head stupidly*)

Her father. (ANNA *looks at him for a minute and then abruptly goes into the cabin, shutting the door. He sits there, forlorn. The cabin door opens and she comes out with a coat on her arm. She throws it over his shoulders.* MAT, *surprised*) Why you doin' this? Ain't you mad?

ANNA

Yeah. But you look cold.

(*Another silence settles between them.* MAT *finally pulls himself together.*)

MAT

Miss. I want to tell you somethin' about me. (*No answer*) Somethin' I wouldn't let nobody else say, neither—or I'd bust his head in. Ask those two guys in there. I don't take nothin' from nobody and I don't go around apologizin', neither. But I'm just gonna tell you, anyways. I'm damn dumb.

ANNA

I shouldn't be surprised.

MAT

(*Shouts*)

Well, I am.

ANNA

I believe you. I'm on your side. And don't yell at me.

(CHRIS *comes out of cabin.*)

47

CHRIS

Dat fella shouldn't be out here still. He should be layin' down.

MAT

I like this better.

CHRIS

Vat's he sayin' to you, Anna?

ANNA

He's just talkin'.

MAT

That's all, Captain. (*Rises slowly*) We're getting to be friendly, that's all—(*Sways*) That's all.
(*He gets up, then falls to the floor in a faint.*)

ANNA
(*Running to him*)

Oh, my God.

CHRIS

Ay take him. (*Calls*) Yonson! Yonson!
(MAT *pulls himself together and sits up.*)

MAT

Let go, let go—

CHRIS

Out on his feets and don't know it.

48

ANNA

You all right?
(JOHNSON *and* SVENSON *enter.*)

MAT

(*Leaning heavily on* JOHNSON *and* SVENSON.)
Sure, I'm all right.

CHRIS

Ve take him inside, Yonson.

MAT

Lemme alone. Lemme alone.

CHRIS

Come on inside, sailor, like Ay say.

ANNA

Go on, get some sleep. We got all day tomorrow to talk.

MAT

All right, good night.
(*Submitting suddenly, with a peaceful smile, he goes to sleep on the deck.*)

Scene 6

A street near the waterfront, bounded on one side by the Seamen's Home. Two proper women, wearing Seamen's Home uniforms and ribbons across their chests, talk excitedly.

MRS. DOWLING

We've got a real nice home-cooked dinner for them.

MRS. SMITH

They'll be here pretty quick now—you see, first the doctor had to examine the men they picked up—that's the law part of it—then the reporters had to get their stories and all that.
(JOHNSON *enters.*)

JOHNSON

I'll tell them.

MRS. SMITH

How they progressing, Johnson?

JOHNSON

They finished with all of us. Now they're takin' pictures.

MRS. SMITH

I'll see if I can hurry things up, Mrs. Dowling.
(*She exits into the Seamen's Home.*)

50

JOHNSON

They got Mat Burke out on the river in a row boat—

MRS. DOWLING

For heaven's sake!

JOHNSON

—and them other two guys layin' down in the bottom.

MRS. DOWLING

(*To Mrs. Smith, who has just returned.*)

This is one of the crew. Will you show him the way, Mrs. Smith?

MRS. SMITH

Aye, aye.

(MRS. SMITH *leads* JOHNSON *out into the home.* CHRIS *and* ANNA *enter.*)

ANNA

(*With temper*)

I don't even want to walk with you.

CHRIS

All dem pictures! Damn foolish.

MRS. DOWLING

Captain, are they on their way?

CHRIS

Yah. Dey come soon.

MRS. DOWLING
(Calling offstage)

Stand ready, girls.

CHRIS

He don't ban sailor anyhow—yust a stoker.

ANNA

Baloney!

CHRIS

Vy don't dey take picture of me? I'm da vun do da rescue.

ANNA

Listen—It don't hurt to be polite.

CHRIS

Polite! I save his life. Dat's polite. Don't I yust give him my shirt?

ANNA

He'll give it back.

CHRIS

I don't vant nodding back. I vant only he should say good-bye. Py golly, next time any sailor fella has shipwreck, I'm gonna hit him across da head vid a oar and push him back in da sea.

ANNA
(Scoffs)

Sure.

52

CHRIS

Vat you say to him all day long ven you sit out dere on deck and talk, talk, talk?

ANNA

Talkin' ain't no harm, is it? Gee whiz, don't you want me to enjoy myself? I never seen a fellow before I like to talk to, like I do him. (*Losing control*) And what the hell business you got tellin' me who I'm talkin' to, anyhow? I got along just fine without you for a long while already.

CHRIS

Anna, dat's no vay for nice gel—

ANNA

Who said I was a nice girl?
  (*She walks away from him to the other side. He follows meekly.*)

CHRIS

Anna—

REPORTER
(*Off-stage*)

Just a second, sailor.

MAT
(*Off-stage*)

No more seconds.

ANNA
(*Abruptly*)

They're comin'.

53

CHRIS

Your poor ole fadder, he don't mean no harm.
(MAT *enters with inquisitive retinue of reporters, photographers, rescued seamen,* MR. SMITH *and hangers-on.*)

ANNA

Sure. Forget it.

REPORTER

But it seems as if you could tell me—

MAT

I told you everythin' I know.

REPORTER

But what I mean is: How did it feel when you were rescued?

MAT

Oh. (*Thinks*) Felt good.

REPORTER

When you realized that you still had a life to live. Come on, something I can use in the paper.

MAT

All right, I'll give you somethin'.
(MRS. SMITH *enters.*)

MRS. SMITH

They can come now.

54

MRS. DOWLING

Wait—he's telling the reporter something.
    (MAT *sings with exaggerated bravado*.)
The sight'd make you sick,
The sharks are gettin' thick.
We're hit by gales 'n bit by whales, just like in *Moby Dick*.
The waves are goin' higher than a mountain,
The whales are blowin' water like a fountain.
   Them two guys in the boat, me up there just rowin'.
Them two guys in the boat, goin', goin', goin'.
Then a blinkin' miracle happens,
Comes a mermaid out of the sea,
Holdin' out 'er hand to me, and

Look at 'er, look at 'er,
Excuse me while I look at 'er,
And melt just like I'm butter in the sun.

Look at 'er, she can't see,
How much she's affectin' me,
I think she's sweet as taffy,
She thinks I'm downright daffy.

Look at me, from the start,
I been chokin' on my heart,
Tastin' words I'm too scared to say,
I'm scared to make a move she wouldn't understand,
I'm scared to smooth 'er hair, or even hold 'er hand,
I know I mustn't touch,
But I don't mind so much,
If I can look at 'er, look at 'er, look at 'er.

CHRIS

Vat kind of sense is all dat talk, huh?

MAT

No sense to it, Captain.

CHRIS

Come on, ve go get someting to eat.

SMITH

Sharks, huh?

SAILOR

And them mermaids, too.

REPORTER

Well, I asked for it and I got it.

SMITH

You sure did.
(*The spectators exit into the Seamen's Home—leaving* MAT *alone.*)

(MAT *sings*)
But now I realize
The reason I have eyes
Is just to look at 'er, look at 'er, look at 'er.

SCENE 7

THE WATERFRONT. *Some girls are dancing with each other, others are sitting around.* SMITH *and* CHRIS *enter through the office.*

SMITH

You've been back two days, huh?

CHRIS

Yah, Mr. Schmidt, Ay ban home two days. Every day dem newspaper fellas come take anodder picture.

SMITH

That's good. The company likes that fine.
(*The* ALDERMAN *and* MRS. SMITH *enter.*)

ALDERMAN

. . . It'll be refined, Mrs. Smith. We have a man at the door to keep out the bad element. But when it comes to politics, I always say, if you've got a vote or two in the family, you're refined. (*Seeing* CHRIS) Ah, Christopherson!
(*He comes to* CHRIS *and gives him tickets.* JOHNSON *carries on a crate, puts it down, scattering the girls.*)

JOHNSON

Gangway.

ALDERMAN

And enjoy yourself, my good man. Now, Mrs. Smith—

CHRIS

(*To the girls*)
Vat you tank? I got two tickets to fancy party.

MOLL

You have?

CHRIS

I take my Anna.

MOLL

Whyn't you take me, Chris?

CHRIS

My daughter Anna.
(CHRIS *exits.*)

ALDERMAN

. . . And you give them out to the finest people you know.

MRS. SMITH

Remember last year, after the ball, how they were singing in
the streets.

ALDERMAN

This year we'll go serenade Tammany Hall.
(MARTHY *enters, wearing a change of sweater, still way
oversized, but of a different color.*)

LILY

Hey, Marthy, you want to know somethin'?

MARTHY

Did you see Chris?

LILY

Did I see him? He was just here. That's what I was going to tell you about. He's got two tickets for the Check Apron Ball. Right there in his hands. Sure thing.

MARTHY

He did? I ain't been to a social function in quite a while.

LILY

You sure he'll ask you?

MARTHY

Ho, ho; if he don't, I'll ask him. I ain't got nothin' proper to wear for such an occasion, but I'll borrow me a needle and thread and fix up a ball gown. I don't need no pattern. I just do it by instinct.

LILY

Maybe he's gonna take that Anna, whatever the hell her name is.

MARTHY

Maybe I already told him a thing or two about that. You should'a heard me.

LILY

You give it to him, huh?

MARTHY

I give you the best years of my life, I says, them that comes after forty-three. And now I don't want to be given no bum's rush, just because you're in the family way.

LILY

That's the stuff, Marthy. (MARTHY *looks offstage*) Oh, here comes the hero.
(MAT *enters.*)

MARTHY

Mornin' to you, Mat Burke.

MAT

Mornin', Marthy.

MARTHY

So long, Lily.

LILY

So long, Marthy. See you in the poorhouse.
(LILY *exits.*)

MAT

You're lookin' pretty as a bunch of roses.
(MARTHY *chuckles at the absurdity of this—then shakes her head.*)

MARTHY

I don't blame her.

60

MAT

Did you see my picture in the paper?

MARTHY

I've seen so many pictures of you in the last couple of days, I'm gettin' bilious. Our hero.

MAT

Yep. A feller down the street wants to tattoo that on me— *Our Hero.*

MARTHY

Whereabouts?

MAT

Huh?

MARTHY

When it comes to tattoos I always claim, it ain't what you say, it's where you put it. I knew a sailor once who—oh, well, never mind . . . (MAT *is looking around for* ANNA. MARTHY *looks up and sees what he is doing*) She ain't here.

MAT

(*Smilingly*)

She will be.

MARTHY

The way you're paradin' around! (*Shakes her head*) Men is peculiar.

MAT

They're always botherin' you, eh, Marthy?

MARTHY

Oh, don't worry, I had plenty of them in my time. Not so long ago, neither. Ho, ho, they was after me. They was killing themselves all over the place. I was quite a thing, you know—gay, merry, up on me toes. It was a terrible strain. So I says to myself, "Marthy Owens, is it worth it? Why don't you relax?" So I quit. I quit cold.

MAT

Have you seen her this mornin'?

MARTHY

You ain't listenin'. Well, the hell with you.

MAT

I'm listenin'.

MARTHY

No, you ain't. Here I am pourin' out me heart's blood. Where is she? he says. Well, I tell you. I guess she's studying her Sunday School lesson, Mat. Or doin' some good deed some place. I don't know. I gotta see a man about a social function.

(*She goes out.*)

(MAT *sings happily.*)
I can't believe this heart is mine,
Inside of me it's singin', gee,
It's good to be alive.

I figured me a hopeless case,
I thought a smile would break my face,
But all along I figured wrong,
It's good to be alive.

Just like a clock, I'd tick and tock,
But nothin' was a kick,
But now I'm glad I'm livin'
'Cause I know what makes me tick.

Now every day I'm feeling more
Of things I never felt before,
I'm in the pink, I'm in the prime,
Just like a kid who found a dime
I'm thinkin', gee, it's good to be alive.
> (ANNA *enters excitedly, followed by a* MASHER, *a sporty type of traveling salesman, dressed to kill.*)

ANNA

Will you go away?
> (*She looks behind her at the* MASHER, *and so does not see* MAT *ahead.*)

MASHER

I ain't pullin' your leg.

ANNA

Go away.

MASHER

Honest, kiddo. I sure seen you somewheres before.

ANNA

You keep the hell away from me, you lousy son of a—(*Turning, she stops short, face to face with* MAT. *Recovers slightly.*) Mat, will you make this man stop following me.
> (THE TWO MEN *look at each other.* MAT *starts toward the* MASHER. THE MASHER *begins to retreat very slowly.*)

MASHER

Hey, now, what's all the fuss? (*He begins to retreat faster as* MAT *increases his pace*) I just—

>   (*He goes running out, and* MAT *runs after him.* ANNA *watches them, goes to some bales in the center of the stage, and sits down, face in her hands, defeated.* MAT *comes back. She looks up.*)

ANNA

You must think I'm awful.

MAT

No, I don't.

ANNA

Talkin' like that, I couldn't hardly believe it was me sayin' it.

MAT

Me, neither.

ANNA

(*With a sudden inspiration*)
Like a farm hand, I guess. Yeah, like a farm hand.

MAT

(*Looking off*)
That guy had some crust. I didn't know they was out in the daytime.

ANNA

They're always out.

64

MAT
(*Darkly—looking off*)
Yellow son—

ANNA

I stopped to look at a store window and he come up beside me and pretended like he knew me from some place else.

MAT

He won't bother you again. (*Softly*) Don't be scared, Anna. I'll take care of you.
(*He takes her arm and she pulls it away quickly.*)

ANNA

Cut it.

MAT

What did I do?

ANNA
(*Angry at herself*)
Nothin'. Nothin'. (*Then, more calmly*) It's just I can't stand fellows grabbin' hold of me.

MAT

But you know how I feel about you. God! Ain't that different?

ANNA

Sure. Sure.

MAT

Listen, Anna, I admire you for bein' choosey. I wouldn't like you if you wasn't.

ANNA

Please, Mat.

MAT

But I do. You ain't got no idea how I feel about you. I worship you.

ANNA

Don't do that. Gee—let's change the subject.

MAT

All right, I will. How do you feel about bein' tattooed?

ANNA

Me?

MAT

No. Me. (*Pointing to his arm*) Right here, Anna! You wouldn't have no objection, would you? (ANNA *shakes her head*) Then no matter where I am in the whole world, you'll be there— And here's another idea. Want to go to a swell affair?

ANNA

A what?

MAT

It's called the Check Apron Ball—an old guy in a high hat give me a couple tickets. On account of the rescue, you know. It's for tomorrow night. How about it?

66

ANNA

(*Abruptly*)

Sure. Why not?

MAT

The sun is shinin' again. Of course, I don't know so much about fancy dancin'.

ANNA

I'll show you.

(*Music starts underneath as* ANNA *draws* MAT *into a dancing position. She leads him hesitantly in a twirl. Gaining confidence quickly, he begins to lead her, and they spin faster and faster around the stage until she is off the ground and in his arms, laughing.*)

Scene 8

The street with the fence. CHRIS *and* MARTHY *enter.*

MARTHY

Why can't you take me? Give one good reason.

CHRIS

'Cause I got odder plan. I vas gonna buy Anna a new red dress and take her to party myself.

MARTHY

Red dress, huh, that's a good idea. Have her carry a lantern.

CHRIS

Vat for, da lantern?

MARTHY

So I can find where you're at.

CHRIS

You can't go, Marthy. You get drunk and say terrible tings.

MARTHY

Why don't you let her feller take her?

CHRIS

She don't got no fella.

68

MARTHY

No. I bet she ain't hardly looked at a man in her life, I bet.

CHRIS

I know vat's right.

MARTHY

So do I! Friendship is right.

CHRIS

Huh?

MARTHY

Listen, Dutchy, maybe I been goin' about this the wrong way. (MARTHY *now speaks more sentimentally*) Friendship, that's sacred. You know that, don't you? That's the unwritten law. We been through a lot together, Dutchy, and don't forget that.

CHRIS

I know, I know.

MARTHY

I say when you got somebody you can count on, that's the thing, that's what I say.
    (*She sings.*)
Yer my friend, ain'tcha, or am I wrong?
And a friend wants a friend to get along,
Friends can have a laugh like strangers never can,
Friends have better fights than strangers ever can.

I'm just right for you, I'm not too smart,
But I'd fight for you, and I'd take your part,

69

So if I call you a squarehead or an s.o.b.,
That's all right for me, I'm yer friend!

CHRIS

(*Quite touched*)
Yah, dat's right, Marthy, dat's right.

MARTHY

So I'll tell you what we'll do. You can get another ticket and
the three of us can all go together.

CHRIS

No! (*Pushes her*) Anna's young innocent gel.

MARTHY

I'm sick of that innocence. Give it a rest, will you, Dutch. We
was all innocent once. I ain't going to say no rough words in
front of her, especially them ones in Swedish you taught me.
(*He starts to walk away. She catches him and holds his arm*)
Wait, Dutchy, I didn't mean nothin'. We're friends, ain't we?

CHRIS

Sure, Marthy, ve friends.

MARTHY

Then leave me just look at the tickets, huh?

CHRIS

Sure, Marthy, you can look.
(*He shows them to her.*)

MARTHY

Oh, they're pretty, ain't they?

CHRIS

Yah.

MARTHY

Well, put them away, and thanks for lettin' me look at them.
You're a real pal.

CHRIS

Ay'm your friend, Marthy.
(*He sings*)
Ve be friends, Marthy, darn tootin' right!
And ve friends, Marthy, even ven ve fight,
Ay'm behind you like a tail dat's on a pup,

(MARTHY)
Okay, Dutchy, you say "make," and I'll say "up,"

(CHRIS)
Make

(MARTHY)
Up
(*They do a little strolling dance, during which she tries to steal a ticket from his pocket.*)

(CHRIS)
Yer yust right for me, you ain't too smart,
But you fight for me, and you take my part,

(MARTHY)
A guy said you ain't fit for pigs down Larry's bar,

(CHRIS)
Vat you say?

(MARTHY)
I said, "Yes you are!"

(CHRIS)
Dat's nice!
Yer my friend!

(BOTH)
Yer my friend, yer my friend, yer my friend!
(She succeeds in extracting the ticket, shows it to him and runs offstage. CHRIS *follows after her, slowly shaking his head.)*

Scene 9

CHRIS'S *room, all bright and gaudy, with mementos of his many journeys across the sea—a Japanese umbrella, an ancient gramophone—and influenced strongly by* MARTHY'S *distinctive feminine touch. Part of the street can be seen.*

ANNA *is holding up her ball dress.* MARTHY *is sitting on the brass bed, her hat off.*

ANNA

No, he came home last night and brought it to me. First thing this mornin', I took it down to the store and changed it for a different color. He'll never notice.

MARTHY

Oh, it's a daisy. A real jumped-up daisy. Very pure, very pure, indeed. A confirmation dress, in a way.

(ANNA *gives her a dirty look and then begins to fold the dress. She stops folding and turns.*)

ANNA

And suppose you just drop all them digs about very pure and all that.

MARTHY

Why, dolly, ain't you sensitive.

73

ANNA

You're damn right I am. So just cheese it. You said you
wanted us to get along.

MARTHY

Well, I do, but I been under a strain lately. It's only human to
be a little peeved when you get the dirty end of the stick like I
have. Damn it all, it ain't fair—a party dress. You know what
he give me last?—these shoes. (*Holds her feet out*) Year before
that he give me this sweater. It ain't so bad, but I had a hell of a
time gettin' the smell of fish out of it.

ANNA

I didn't ask him for nothin'.

MARTHY

There ain't no justice.

ANNA

And, geez, when he found out I was going' to this ball with
Mat, he yelled bloody murder. He sure is a funny old guy.

MARTHY

He keeps me laughin'— What good jokes has he said lately?
    (ANNA *gives her a look of rebuke.*)

ANNA

Aw, come on.
    (MARTHY *placates her.*)

74

MARTHY

No, no, kiddo, don't get sore. I ain't got used to this business yet, that's all. Well, it won't last forever, you'll team up with Mat most likely and get a place of your own.

ANNA

Not if my father has his way. He don't want no fellows around at all, do you know that. Ain't that nutty?

MARTHY

That's the way it is. They're all like that. All fathers is stinkers. It's the way nature works things out—they make themselves so damn disagreeable, you go off with some other man just to get away from home.
(MAT *is seen coming down the street.*)

ANNA

You certainly don't take life serious, do you, Marthy? Don't nothin' ever bother you? I mean about mistakes a person makes. Can you forget them things? Can you change? (*There's a knock on the door. She lowers her voice*) Who could that be?

MARTHY

There's one way to find out. (*Yells*) Who is it?

MAT

(*Outside door*)

Me. Mat.
(ANNA *rushes to the door and opens it, then she pauses.*)

ANNA

Come in.
> (MAT *enters and sees* MARTHY.)

MAT

I thought maybe you was alone.

MARTHY
> (*Rising*)

She is. (*Picks up her hat*) Tell the old squarehead I'll see him at the ball.

ANNA
> (*Surprised*)

You will?

MARTHY

Oh, I know I ain't supposed to go. I was given my order. "You'll get drunk and disgrace my little Anna," he says. But we know there's no sense to that. I got a ticket and Marthy Owen can mix with high-toned folks as well as the best of them. (*Begins to act out the part*) You just peek from behind your fan— step dainty and lay off the booze. It's tricky, but I can do it. (*To* MAT) How do you like this hat, sailor?

MAT
> (*Absently*)

Fine.

MARTHY

That's what I think. Shows I ain't tryin' to put on the dog.
> (*She goes out.*)

MAT

She's crazy. (*Shows tattoo*) How do you like it?

ANNA

(*Touched*)

Oh, Mat!

MAT

It's on there forever—see?

ANNA

Mat.

MAT

Now, if you want it fixed up fancier, I can have them put some doves on with ribbons, you know.

ANNA

Oh, no, leave it just the way it is. (*Changing the subject*) How do you like my dress?

MAT

I like everythin' about you. (*Blurting out*) How do I stand? Come on now, tell me. Anna, I ain't touched a hand to you, like you asked. But you know how much I love you. And I think you feel the same way about me. But I got to find out; I got to be sure.

ANNA

(*Very still*)

I been thinkin' and thinkin' (*Looks up*) I didn't want to, Mat, I'll own up to that. But I guess I can't help it. So I do.

77

Sure, I do. What's the use of kiddin' myself different. Sure I do love you, Mat.

MAT

Anna.

ANNA

And I ain't loved a man in my life before. You can always believe that, no matter what happens.

MAT

I believe you, darlin'. (*They kiss*) Oh, God! (*They kiss again.* MAT *sings*)
Open your eyes, open your eyes,
Where were you, where were you?

(ANNA)
I was on a pretty island,
Somewhere on a shiny sea,
You were with me on the island,
Where I wanted you to be.

(BOTH)
Did you close your eyes when we kissed?
Did you close your eyes when we kissed?
Did you close your eyes when we kissed, like me?

(MAT)
I just floated straight to heaven
Countin' angels while I flew,
Though I counted six or seven,
Angel, all of them were you.
My eyes are wide open and yet,
I still see through kind of a mist.

(BOTH)

Did you close your eyes when we kissed, like me?
Did you close your eyes when we kissed?
Did you close your eyes when we kissed?
Did you close your eyes when we kissed, like me,
   like me, like me?

(*They kiss at the end of the song.* CHRIS *enters and is startled to see* MAT *there. He closes the door slowly.* MAT *takes* ANNA's *hand.*)

MAT

You come just in time to get the good news. I'm goin' to marry your daughter.

CHRIS

Vat? Vat is dis, Anna?

ANNA

Mat.

MAT

Yes, darlin'.

ANNA

I only said—

MAT

You said you loved me—and I love you—and we'll get married—and I'll save my money and never look at another woman —and we'll have little devils of boys and girls runnin' all over the place—(*Turns to Chris*) Now, Grandpop, what's the matter with that?

79

CHRIS

She don't marry vid no sailor fella.

MAT

Oh, don't she? You know what's the trouble with you—you don't want her to marry nobody.

CHRIS

Listen, you fella, Ay'm ole man. She vas all Ay got in vorld. And now she come on first trip, you tank Ay vant be left alone again. You go vay—you got gel in every port—you know dat, you'll soon forget Anna.

MAT

Shut up! I'll never forget her, not till I'm dead. She's the one woman in the whole world for me.

CHRIS

Ay don't know vy you make all dis trouble—don't Ay save your life?

MAT

No—I saved my own life—rowin' with my two hands. If that scow of yours hadn't been in the way, I'd a-rowed to shore. You're probably scared of the sea, or you wouldn't be on a lousy barge.

CHRIS

You coal-heaver.

MAT

Well, get one thing straight. I'm marryin' your daughter.

80

CHRIS

Never, never, never.

MAT

Anna, will you tell the man.

ANNA

Mat, if I'd knowed you two years ago. But I can't do it to you—I can't do it.

MAT

I don't know what you're sayin'.

ANNA

I said I loved you, but I didn't say I'd marry you.

MAT

But you got to marry me.

CHRIS

She don't vant to.

MAT

She does.
(*Each of them takes one of* ANNA's *arms, and they pull her back and forth.*)

ANNA

(*Angrily, shaking loose*)
Will you shut up, the both of you. Fightin' over me like I was some kind of a animal—like I didn't have nothin' to say. Nothin' don't last, I guess. (*Picking up ball dress*) Well,

thanks for the dress, anyways. (*Throws the dress on floor, stifling a cry of pain.*)

CHRIS

(*Picking up dress*)

Anna!

ANNA

Take it back and get your money.

CHRIS

You ain't gonna vear dress?

ANNA

Where to? We can't go to no ball like this—fightin'.

CHRIS

It vas yust little argument. Now ve go to ball like good friends—ve fight tomorrow.

ANNA

(*Goes to* CHRIS *and takes back dress—hopefully*)

Yeah? Tomorrow? We decide all these things tomorrow? Huh, Mat?

MAT

Whatever you say.

ANNA

Huh, Father?

CHRIS

Yeah, sure.

ANNA

Tonight everybody is supposed to be happy, that's what I say.

A street scene, made festive because the street is lined with various colored discarded doors linked together to form a wall. Overhead there is a network of telephone lines.

>   (*Gaily dressed revelers cross on their way to the Check Apron Ball, singing*)

Here comes my passion,
Lookin' absolutely dashin',
The height of fashion
For the big Check Apron Ball,

Look out for Celia,
If she tries to chicken-reel ya,
She's out to steal ya,
At the big Check Apron Ball,

Oh, in these modern days,
When ladies show their ankles,
What's there to keep a poor lad,
From goin' simply mad?
We haven't told 'em,
But we're makin' sure we hold 'em,
We'll just blindfold 'em,
At the big Check Apron Ball.

Mother, Mother, don't wait up for me, don't worry!
Mother, Mother, let me have the key, won't hurry,

Won't be home till three, see,
Skin-a-ma-rink, skin-a-ma rink, skin-a-ma-rinky dink.
Mother, Mother, though I hate to brag, I thrill 'em,
'Specially when I do the Jersey rag, I kill 'em,
Then I holler hey! hey!
Skin-a-ma-rink, skin-a-ma-rink away.

Hutzum, putzum, Egypt is the nutsum, oh, the way they
   dance!
Poor lad! From goin' simply mad?
Oh, Mother, nowadays the girls are awful wild, those women!
How ya gonna keep your honeychild from sinnin'?
Catch me if I fall, boom!
Gotta get to, I gotta get to, I gotta get to,
Gotta get to, I gotta get to, I gotta get to,
I gotta get to, I gotta get to, I gotta get to;
I gotta get to, I gotta get to, I gotta get to,
I gotta get to the ball.

Scene 11

The ball.

The brewery has been decorated in great style for the event. At the back there is a raised level, where they probably load beer at some time, but now chairs and tables have been placed there so the people sitting can watch the dancing in the foreground.

Waiters, in loud check aprons, go back and forth carrying trays of liquor which they pass to anyone who wants a drink. We see MARTHY *stepping daintily and looking at people over her fan. Her dress is a makeshift business, and she's wearing the same old men's shoes. People are standing around in small groups.*

SMITH

Well, Larry. I didn't know you ever touched it.

LARRY

Well, tonight I thought I'd celebrate. Here's to the Alderman.

MRS. SMITH

. . . And the most beautiful music.

WAITER

(*Coming up behind* MARTHY)

Drink, lady?

MARTHY

(*Brusquely*)

Not on your life. (*Quickly controls herself and gets coy*) I mean, I seldom touch it.

(*A little to her left, the* ALDERMAN *is talking to* MRS. HAM-MACHER, MR. *and* MRS. DOWLING *and others.*)

ALDERMAN

. . . And it's lovely ladies like yourself that make it so.

DOWLING

Well, I do think it's a great success.

(MARTHY *sidles up to them.*)

MRS. DOWLING

I do, too.

MRS. HAMMACHER

I do, too.

MARTHY

(*Trying to get in on the act and be sociable*)

I do, too.

(*They look at her. She returns the glance coyly over her fan.* MRS. HAMMACHER *turns aside coldly and leads the* MEN *away.*)

MRS. DOWLING

I suppose you're going to vote for me for queen of the ball, Alderman.

(*Another waiter approaches* MARTHY.)

WAITER

What'll it be?

MARTHY

Absolutely nothin'. Take your nasty alcohol to some of them that needs it.

(*As she is posing self-righteously,* LARRY *passes by. He turns and looks at her.*)

LARRY

Well, well, well!

MARTHY

What's the matter with you? Have you never seen a lady at a ball?

LARRY

So they let you in.

MARTHY

I wouldn't even of come if I'd known they was goin' to invite bartenders.

LARRY

And their best customers, eh, Marthy?

MARTHY

That's where you missed it by a mile. (*To a* WAITER *who has passed her a tray*) Pass me by, man; don't loiter.

88

LARRY

(*Goes away laughing*)

Marthy, you're a killer.

(OSCAR, PETE *and* SVENSON *enter, like three lone wolves. They are peering at all the girls.*)

OSCAR

They got cartloads of good-lookers here tonight.

PETE

This one is a peacherino.

SVENSON

It's old Chris' daughter.

OSCAR

The blonde is?

SVENSON

Sure.

PETE

We'll get him to give us a knockdown.

(MAT *and* ANNA *enter and cross toward the center of the stage.*)

MAT

I thought I was goin' to be alone with you.

ANNA

Well, gee, Mat, I . . .

MAT

Ever since we got here—pleased to meet you this one—pleased to meet you that—

ANNA

But you was the one that wanted to come, Mat.

MAT

Well, that ain't no lie. I guess I ain't very polite.

ANNA

You suit me.

MAT

Let's not stay here forever, huh? (*Looks off right as* CHRIS *enters*) Oh, look out, here comes the trouble.
(*He leads her away.*)

CHRIS
(*To one of the guests*)

Sure, my Anna.

POLITICIAN
(*Seeing* MAT)

Ah, there's our hero.

MAT

My friend, Miss Christopherson.

POLITICIAN

Charmed, I'm sure.

90

MARTHY

(*Observing*)

Oh, for Pete's sake. It's disgustin'.

CHRIS

Oh, sure, Anna, she like to make acquaintance of my friends.
(*A waiter stands beside* MARTHY *with a tray of drinks.*)

MARTHY

I never touch the stuff.

ANNA

. . . Out where we live.
(*Laughter from the group around her.*)

MARTHY

Listen to them. It's enough to drive you . . . (*She smells a drink on the tray. A woman approaches and* MARTHY *addresses her*) I seldom touch the stuff. (*She looks at a drink, scratches her back coyly with her fan, and finally sips it. This is the end. She tosses it off and sets the empty glass on the tray*) It's the kind of thing that could happen to anybody. (*The waiter starts off and she stops him*) Waiter! You goin' to a fire? I come in on a ticket, same as the rest of them.
(*She drinks another.*)

OSCAR

(*Pushing aside other men near* ANNA)

Hold your horses, Pete, I asked her first.
(LARRY *takes* MARTHY *aside.*)

LARRY

Hey, don't I know her?

MARTHY

The one with the halo?

LARRY

The blonde. Ain't she the one?—

MARTHY

Mum's the word. But—I could say a thing or two.

LARRY

What?

MARTHY

Mum's the word.

LARRY

You're gettin' quite a snootful, ain't you, Marthy?

MARTHY

I ain't pretendin' to be better than I am, like some people.

OSCAR

No, we don't want a waltz—we want ragtime.

MARTHY

I'm no hypocrite. I think any woman that's got the spark of life should have a snifter of beer once in a while—or a shot of bourbon—or just somethin' to give her breath a smell. (*Takes drink from* LARRY) Want to dance?

(She grabs his shoulders and he has difficulty shaking her off. Another waiter passes her. She lets out a shrill whistle and follows him off.)

ALDERMAN

Miss Christopherson, may I have the honor?
(The ALDERMAN *gives* ANNA *his arm, inviting her to dance. They take the center of the room.)*

OSCAR

You can pick 'em, Alderman.

CHRIS

My Anna, she's da best vun here.

MAT

What arc they goin' to do?

SVENSON

He'll sing it out.

PETE

Come on, Alderman, lead it off.

ALDERMAN

I'll do that.

ALL

Hooray!

LARRY

Sing it, Clancy.

(*The* ALDERMAN *sings*)
Angelo Galoopy was a barber,
All the way from sunny Italy,
Had a little shop down in the harbor,
Near the Statue of Liberty—hooray!
When the good time sports that hung around inside,
Kidded Angelo and hurt his pride,
Angelo would bet a bowlful of spaghett,
He was just as flashy as they, he'd say:

(CHORUS)
When I get dressed, in all my best,
There ain't no flies on me,
I win every prize,
I ain't got no flies,
Dogs bow wow, cats meow,
When they have a flea,
But there ain't no flies on me!

(POLITICIAN)
Everybody's friend is Charley Clancy,
Alderman down in the fourteenth ward,
Don't think Mister Clancy,
Doesn't dress up fancy,
He wears clothes the mayor can't afford—Oh,

(CHORUS)
Oh,
When I get dressed, in all my best,
There ain't no flies on me,

I win every prize,
I ain't got no flies,
Dogs bow wow, cats meow,
When they have a flea,
But there ain't no flies on me!

(LARRY)
Everybody here knows Olie Olsen,
He works on a barge that goes toot-toot!
Ain't much on a Monday,
But you should see him Sunday,
When he takes a shave and wears a suit—**Oh,**

(CHORUS)
When I get dressed, in all my best,
There ain't no flies on me,
I win every prize,
I ain't got no flies,
Dogs bow wow, cats meow,
When they have a flea,
But there ain't no flies on
Ain't no flies
Ain't no flies
Ain't no flies on me.

> (*Dancing follows. First,* ANNA *and two of the sailors do a soft shoe; then the entire assemblage; and then* ANNA *lets her hair down and dances her joy at finally being accepted. All of the guests high step to a cake walk.*)

Curtain

ACT TWO

ACT TWO

Scene 1

As the curtain rises, the guests are high-kicking, just as they were at the end of Act One. ANNA *is dancing in the center of the stage. Only a second has elapsed. At the end of the dance, the guests surround* ANNA.

POLITICIAN

My dear, you must have wings on your feet. Light as a feather, you are.

ANNA

Well, thanks.

POLITICIAN

I must introduce you to Senator Malone. (MARTHY *enters drunkenly*) He can step it out with the best of them.

ANNA

I always did like dancin'.

POLITICIAN

Where did you learn, my dear?

ANNA

Oh, out West, mostly.

99

MARTHY

(*As* WAITER *passes*)

Oh, waiter! Slow down when you pass by me. You must be new around here. (*Drinks*) This ain't no way station. This is a permanent stop.

(CHRIS *comes up to* MARTHY.)

CHRIS

Marthy, you vant everybody lookin' at you?

MARTHY

Let them look.

CHRIS

Vat people gonna tank?

MARTHY

It ain't none of your business what they think.

CHRIS

Vy don't you yust keep quiet?

MARTHY

Oh, shut up.

CHRIS

Now, Marthy.

MARTHY

Just mind your own damn business.

100

CHRIS

People lookin'.

MARTHY

I got no connection with you no more—nor your snooty daughter, neither. I've left you, see, I've left you flat.

ALDERMAN

(*Comes forward to calm the troubled waters*)
Ain't it a little early?

MARTHY

(*Abashed*)

What?

ALDERMAN

The fightin' don't generally start 'til later in the evenin'.

CHRIS

I told you.

ALDERMAN

Now, now—the both of you. We all want to get along together, ain't that right—and set a good example.

MARTHY

I'm a good example.

ALDERMAN

Yes, you are, dear. And now we're gonna have a little dance, and you and Christopherson can lead it off.

MARTHY

Let his daughter lead it off. She's the one.

OSCAR

Yeah, get the daughter.

MRS. DOWLING

Which one is that?

PETE

Where's Anna?

SVENSON

(Calling)

Miss Christopherson.

MARTHY

She's with him. I'm only here on a ticket.

ALDERMAN

But you're happy now.

MARTHY

Ho—oh, I'm laughin' my head off.

OSCAR

Here she is!

SVENSON

Play a waltz.

PETE

Come on, Anna.

SVENSON

You show 'em, Captain.

POLITICIAN

Can the man dance at all?

ALDERMAN

Step it out, now, Miss Christopherson. I'm countin' on you.

    (CHRIS *sings*)
Ven ve valse,

    (ANNA)
Yumpty, dumpty dum,

    (CHRIS)
Ven ve valse,

    (ANNA)
Yumpy, dumpy dum,

    (BOTH)
When we waltz, when we waltz, then we got 'em.

    (ANNA)
First we glide, then we glide like a feather,

    (CHRIS)
Dese are vings on our feet, not shoe ledder.
Dere are girls vat don't tank I'm good lookin'
Dere are girls vat don't tank I'm so smart,

    (ANNA)
But—

(CHRIS)
Ven ve valse

(ANNA)
Yumpy, dumpy dum,
When we waltz,

(CHRIS)
Yumpy, dumpy dum,

(ANNA)
Them same girls just tear him apart.
(*They lead the guests in a waltz.*)

(ANNA)
When we waltz,

(CHORUS)
Yumpy, dumpy dum,

(ANNA)
When we waltz,

(CHORUS)
Yumpy, dumpy dum,

(ANNA)
When we waltz, when we waltz, we're the bestes'.
We keep slidin' and glidin' and pumpin',
We're right there till the last umpeh's umpin'.

(CHRIS)
You may tank dere's no steam in my boiler,

(ANNA)
You may say, "Look, he wobbles, and jerks,"
But when we waltz,

104

(CHORUS)
Yumpy, dumpy dum,

(ANNA)
When we waltz,

(CHORUS)
Yumpy, dumpy dum,

(BOTH)
You see the machinery works.
   (*The men at the ball cut in on* CHRIS *and on each other to
   dance with* ANNA.)

(CHORUS)
When they waltz, yumpy dumpy dum,
When they waltz, yumpy dumpy dum,
When they waltz, when they waltz, they're the bestes'.
First they slide, then they glide like a feather,
They got wings on their feet, not shoe leather.
Every twirl, every whirl is a picture,
Like these eyes never gazed at before,
When they waltz, yumpy, dumpy dum,
When they waltz, yumpy, dumpy dum,
You just got to give 'em
You just got to give 'em
You just got to give 'em the floor.
   (*The waltz ends.* MARTHY *staggers on, even drunker,
   bumping into* OSCAR.)

SAILOR

Hey! Grab her.

MARTHY

Let me go. (ANNA *and the* ALDERMAN *cross in front of* MARTHY)
Speak to me, you stuck-up thing.

    (MAT, *watching from the sidelines, crosses to* MARTHY.)

MAT

Marthy, what the hell kind of a way is that to be actin'?

MARTHY

Some day you'll find out.

MAT

Why don't you go home and sleep it off?

MARTHY

If I want to sleep, I got plenty of places around here. Two of
my friends slept here last year. You know—Mrs. McCloskey,
Black eyed Betsy and her sister, Two-dollar Lillie?

MAT

I'm going to take you downstairs and—

    (*He tries to guide her; she wrenches free.*)

MARTHY

Take your hands off me or I'll tell you a thing or two—so
pure in her damn white dress. I can't bear it.

MAT

Shut up. You're so low you—

MARTHY

I may be low but I got company.

106

MAT

You hear me—

MARTHY

Some of them that's pretendin' to be so high and mighty. I ain't so dumb as some people. I can tell a nurse from a sportin' lady a long way off.

MARTHY

What did you say?

MARTHY

Let go.

MAT

All right now, what did you say?

MAT

I don't know what I said. I'm a little dizzy. Somethin' foolish, no doubt.
(*She falls in a faint in the center of the ballroom. The proper ladies gasp.*)

LARRY

Take it easy, ladies, take it easy. All right boys, give us a hand. (*They lift her*) We better take this out in the air before she messes up the place.
(*They do.* ANNA *enters and crosses to* MAT.)

ANNA

Mat. (*He pulls away from her reach*) Mat.
(*She is perplexed until he pulls away from her again and looks at her. In horror she turns and runs off.*)

Scene 2

In the street, outside the brewery. ANNA *enters;* MAT *follows.*

MAT

What did you run away for?

ANNA

I didn't run away, Mat.

MAT

I'm askin' you—why did you sneak out on me?

ANNA

I didn't sneak. I just got away from you because I didn't like the way you was actin'. You wasn't bein' very pleasant and I just moved away from you, that's all, cause I didn't know what else to do. Gee whiz, Mat, I never seen you like that before.

MAT

You ran to hide. I could see it. You been lyin' to me, ain't you? All about what kind of a person you was and everythin'. You been laughin' up your sleeve at me. You're makin' a fool of me.

ANNA

No, Mat. I wouldn't do that.

108

MAT

Well, what have you got to say?

ANNA

What do you want me to say, Mat?

MAT

Marthy told me.

ANNA

Told you what? And you believed her? Is that what you do, just go round believin' what every foolish old drunk's goin' to tell you?

MAT

All right. You tell me. Well, what're you goin' to tell me?

ANNA

I don't know, Mat.

MAT

No, I suppose you ain't quite decided yet. Here I am bein' made to feel wicked because I took hold of your arm, and you already been goin' around with a lot of guys. Well, do you deny it? Do you?

ANNA

Yes.

MAT

Anna.

ANNA

(*Violently*)

No!

MAT

Huh?

ANNA

It ain't no use.

MAT

What ain't?

ANNA

I told you you was the only man I ever loved. That's true. No matter what happens—no matter what you think—that's true. I done wrong things, and I done right things. Ain't that just like everybody? (*Desperately*) Can't a person change?

MAT

All right—how many?

ANNA

You standin' up there like a judge in a court askin' me questions—Have you been perfect?

MAT

Never mind me.

ANNA

Where have you been? I guess I know. Battin' around in the joints of every dirty waterfront in the world. But I got to be spotless. Well, I ain't. I got to give you the answers. All right.

Yes. Yes. I had men. Worse than you think. But I hated them, every one of them. What if I done bad things? Ain't there no reasons? I was alone. I was hungry. I wasn't no nurse, the last two years. I was in a house. You know what kind of a house. You've been in plenty of them. (MAT *grabs her. She speaks hysterically*) Now go ahead and beat me, like you're goin' to. Kill me, I don't care.

MAT

You slut—(*He throws her brutally on the floor*)—you dirty— You! One of them. Why don't I kill you—why don't I kill you dead?

ANNA

(*Sobbing*)

Do it! Do it!

MAT

God help me, I'll never believe in nobody again so long as I live.

ANNA

Get out, go on, get out!

MAT

I'll get out. And you'll never see me again—I'll go so far away I can forget you forever.

(*He rushes out. Laughter is heard offstage.* ANNA *gets up and hides in the shadows.*)

ALDERMAN

(*Off-stage*)

Come on, we'll take a little walk.

POLITICIAN
(*Off-stage*)

Good idea, Charlie.

ALDERMAN
(*As he and* POLITICIAN *enter*)

They're havin' a good time.

POLITICIAN

We can get a bit of air.

ALDERMAN

You've got to give the voters jobs, but, you've also got to give them entertainment, and we're doin' it.

POLITICIAN

This one is a wing-ding. I vote it the best.
(CHRIS *enters, looking for* ANNA.)

ALDERMAN

Christopherson. Are you enjoyin' yourself?

CHRIS

Dat damn Marthy, she got drunk.

ALDERMAN

It happens to the best of us.

CHRIS

Dat vat she said.
(ALDERMAN *and* POLITICIAN *go out, mumbling.*)

OSCAR
(*Off-stage*)
It's a wing-ding of a party, Alderman.
(CHRIS *peers into the gloom, looking for* ANNA.)

CHRIS

Anna?

ANNA

Yes?

CHRIS

You all right?

ANNA

Sure.

CHRIS

Vat you doin'?

ANNA

Gettin' a bit of air.

CHRIS

Dat Senator Malone, he vants to dance vid you. (*She starts out*) Vere you goin'?

ANNA

For a walk.
(*She exits hurriedly.*)

A street in the warehouse district, late at night. KRIMP, *a shifty waterfront operator, and three sailors enter.*

KRIMP

Ah, you're going to like it, lads. First port is Honolulu—them babies is right there on the beach with their arms stretched out. And the next stop—wait—where the hell's that other fella? (*Calls offstage*) Hey, come on. (MAT *enters, disheveled*) Thought we'd lost you.

MAT

Just stopped for a drink.

KRIMP

Another one?

MAT

Yeah—another one. Got any objections?

KRIMP

No, pal. I just don't want to lose you, that's all.

MAT

'Cause if you have, just say so, and I'll knock the teeth down your ugly throat—and that goes for the rest of you, too.

KRIMP

We gotta sail with the tide. This *Eastward Ho* is a sweet little ship.

MAT

Nobody wants a sweet little ship. I want a sour ship—I want a lousy ship—(LILY, MARTHY *and* PEARL *enter, overhear him*) That's what they all call it—the lousy *Eastward Ho*.
(MAT, KRIMP *and sailors exit.*)

LILY

Did you see who that was, Marthy?

MARTHY

I seen it.

LILY

Lover's quarrel—sure as hell.
(MARTHY *groans sickly.*)

PEARL

Take it easy, Marthy.

LILY

He's just goin' to forget her—off to the briny deep.

MARTHY

It's sad. And it's all my fault.

PEARL

Now don't start that again.

MARTHY

Did you ever have somethin' pressin' on your brain, huh, Lily? Huh, Pearl? I got somethin' pressin' on my brain. I done somethin' terrible and I don't want to remember it. . . . That's why I don't want to get too sober.

LILY

You ain't in no danger at the moment.

MARTHY

I didn't mean to get drunk. I never touch the stuff, I says.

LILY

You didn't say it loud enough.

MARTHY

But they kept at me and at me. First I'd see her in her damn white dress with everybody bowin' around—and then they'd pass a whole trayful of the stuff—

(ANNA *enters. She comes forward and takes a long look at* MARTHY.)

MARTHY

(*Hanging her head*)

Anna, I was jealous.

ANNA

(*Coldly*)

Have you seen Mat?

116

MARTHY

(*Suddenly*)

Anna, deny it—that's all you gotta do—look him right in the eye and deny it.

ANNA

Where is he?

LILY

Dearie, to tell you the truth, he's headed straight for China.

ANNA

What?

LILY

They'll be coming back this way. They just went up to the ship's office.

ANNA

Oh.

(*She exits.*)

MARTHY

(*To* LILY *and* PEARL)

You know somethin'—I'm rotten clean through.

LILY

No, Marthy. Not all the way.

(*Weary revelers enter.*)

MARTHY

Yes I am. (PEARL, *supporting* MARTHY, *begins leading her offstage*) You'll see. You'll see.

(The group from the ball increases. OSCAR *sings)*
One sweet day she left her dear old mammy,

(OSCAR *and* PETE)
Sweet potatoes and her southern hammy.

(LARRY)
Some of us win and some of us lose,

(ALL THREE)
Some get the prize and some get the blues.
       (MARTHY, PEARL *and* LILY *exit. A policeman enters.*)

(CHORUS)
He gave her kisses 'n promised the moon,
But now he's singin' a different tune.
He left her waitin' alone at the church,
He left her waitin' alone in the lurch.
With all her broken dreams it's no surprise,
The Sunshine Girl has raindrops in her eyes.

You hear them fallin' a-pitter 'n pat,
She wears a rain cloud instead of a hat,
She still remembers the day that they met,
She may forgive him but never forget.
An angel's heart became the devil's prize,
The Sunshine Girl has raindrops in her eyes.
The Sunshine Girl has raindrops in her eyes.
       (They exit. ANNA *reappears, and voices are heard offstage.*
       She hides behind a gate as sailors pass.)

FIRST SAILOR
. . . All the way to Hongkong and we didn't get ashore.

SECOND SAILOR

I shipped out with that second mate before. What a skunk.

FIRST SAILOR

I don't mind if they give you decent shore leave. Get a good skipper and it ain't bad.

THIRD SAILOR

It's a job.
(*They exit as* MAT *enters, walking disconsolately.*)

ANNA

(*Coming out from behind the gate*)

Mat.

MAT

Are you a ghost?

ANNA

No, I'm Anna.

MAT

I can see you all right. I've been drinkin' but I can't get drunk.

ANNA

Mat, before you go—

MAT

I can see you plain. Sure, I see you.

ANNA

I can't bear it . . .

MAT

It's the slut, all right.

ANNA

Maybe I was, Mat, but I ain't any more. Can't you believe me? Don't you see I'm tellin' you the truth?

MAT

Sure, same as you did all of them others. Lies.

ANNA

It's not a lie.

MAT

It's a lie. (*Singing voices are heard offstage*) Same as you told a hundred times. All lies.

ANNA

You don't think I was in love with them. Not one of them. Not a single one.

MAT

Every one of them. All of them. All of them. All of them.

ANNA
(*Turning*)

Good-bye, Mat.
(*She exits.*)

MAT

(*Shouting*)

All of them.

(MARTHY *enters, followed by* LILY *and* PEARL. MARTHY *comes forward.*)

MARTHY

Oh, Mat! Mat! I was lookin' for you. I was afraid you took that joke of mine too serious . . .

MAT

Get out of my way.

(MAT *pushes* MARTHY *aside angrily, and exits.* MARTHY *sways. The women come to her.*)

MARTHY

I done a lot of mean things in my life, but I never sunk as low as this before. If I thought it'd do any good, I'd cut my throat. They ought to hang me for what I done to that girl. I'm gonna pay the price. I'm gonna take the pledge.

(LILY *and* PEARL *laugh raucously at this new absurdity.*)

CHRIS'S *room.* CHRIS *sits on his bed.* ANNA *is lying down, facing away from him.*

CHRIS

Ay tank you should talk to me. Your fadder ban friend. He vant only you should be nice—happy. Vat makes you cry? Huh, Anna? Vy you valkin' around alone in de streets two o'clock in de morning? (SVENSON *is seen outside. He knocks.* CHRIS *goes to door, puts his finger to his lips and comes out*) Sh! Yeah?

(ANNA *sits up, gets a beat-up carpetbag from across the room, and begins to pack.*)

SVENSON

We got everythin' aboard, Captain.

CHRIS

I come—right avay—I come. (CHRIS *returns to the door and opens it quietly*) Anna, vhy don't you come vid me on barge. Sunshine, fresh air, good grub—you feel good in couple days.

ANNA

I gotta be by myself. I gotta think.

CHRIS

Vhy you didn't come back to party, Anna? People look for you. You vas best vun dere, dat vat dey all say.

ANNA

(*In a level voice*)
Well, you see, Father—I wasn't the best one there.

CHRIS

Yah, da qveen, dat's vat da Alderman say, da qveen.

ANNA

You better stop talkin' like that, you might make a fool out of yourself. (ANNA *sits down*) Marthy can tell you some different things—and maybe others.

CHRIS

You yust right, Anna—you yust right for your fadder. Ay gotta go now, Anna. Dey vait for me.

ANNA

Have a good trip.

CHRIS

Anna, you take care of yourself.

ANNA

I will, Father.

CHRIS

(*Quietly*)
You ban de best vun.
(*He exits.*)

(ANNA *sits and sings*)
They talk about the feelin',

How something in you rings,
You fly around the ceilin'
'Cause love can give you wings.
The ringing is a lie,
I didn't learn to fly,
If that was love, love hurts an awful lot.

> (ANNA *comes out of the bedroom carrying her bag, and as
> she walks downstage she resumes singing*)

Unless somebody cares once,
They say it's awful sad.
I stumbled down the stairs once,
It didn't hurt as bad.
If love can give you wings,
And something in you sings,
Then maybe love just wasn't what I got,
If that was love, it hurt an awful lot.

> (*The street with the fence moves into place behind* ANNA.
> HENRY, *a big, lumbering farmer, enters, calls to her.*)

HENRY

Miss. Miss. Are you all right?

> (*She doesn't answer, but turns upstage. The street disap-
> pears, and in her mind* ANNA *sees a group of ladies of the
> evening sprawled lazily in a brothel.* ANNA *joins them,
> and in a ballet relives the experience with the* MASHER,
> *who carries her upstairs to the derisive laughter of the
> ladies. At the end of the ballet the street comes back into
> place, and* ANNA *picks up her bag as* HENRY *reappears.*)

HENRY

Miss . . . are you all right?

ANNA

Yes.

HENRY

Thought maybe somethin' was wrong. This ain't a very nice street for a lady like you.

ANNA

A lady like me?

HENRY

I mean, at this hour and all. Maybe I'd better escort you back to the main street.

ANNA

Yes, I'd like that.

HENRY

I run a little produce business and sell things around this neighborhood.
(*He leads the way offstage.*)

ANNA

(*Gratefully, and with newly discovered self-respect*)
Yes, I'd like that very much.
(*She follows him off.*)

SCENE 5

The waterfront.
One year later.
The ALDERMAN *is again giving out tickets to the ball.*

MRS. SMITH

Are you going to have it again this year?

ALDERMAN

Every year, my dear lady. You can always count on it. We show our appreciation to our loyal voters.

SVENSON
(*Entering with* CHRIS)
. . . Oh, it wasn't so bad, Captain.

ALDERMAN

And, will you be there, my dear?

MRS. SMITH

Alderman, I wouldn't miss it.

CHRIS

Did you see Anna, Mr. Schmidt?

SMITH

No, but I expect she'll be around pretty soon. This is Wednesday. That's one of her days, isn't it?

CHRIS

Yeah, she come on Vednesday.

SMITH

She like it over there on Staten Island with Henry?

CHRIS

I don't know, Mr. Schmidt—but she goot gel . . . and dat fella Henry nice fella. Come on, Svenson, ve go drink by Larry's.
(ROSE, *one of the tarts, crosses to* CHRIS.)

ROSE

Hello, Chris. I just saw a friend of yours. You know, that fellow you rescued last year.

CHRIS

Vat you say?

ROSE

Remember? His picture was in the papers . . . Mat Burke.

CHRIS

Ay tought he vas gone to China.

ROSE

I don't know where he was gone, but he's back. Cute gazabo. Got a ring in his ear. I seen him down by the dock.
(*She exits.*)

ALDERMAN

Ah, Christopherson, you'll be wantin' to go to the Check Apron Ball again this year . . .

CHRIS

(*Distracted*)

Tanks.

ALDERMAN

. . . And here's a pair of tickets for your lovely daughter.

CHRIS

Yeah, tanks.

SVENSON

Come on, Chris.

CHRIS

You go.

SVENSON

What?

CHRIS

Someting happen. Ay vait here.

SVENSON

You all right, Captain?

CHRIS

Ay can't tank vat to do. (*Mat enters behind and listens unnoticed*) Dat fella Mat Burke is back again. Ay don't vant he should find my Anna.

MAT

He ain't even looking for her. (CHRIS *jumps up and whirls around*) What a fearful man you are—just like old times. Hello, Svenson.

SVENSON

Hello, Mat.

CHRIS

Vy you don't stay in China?

MAT

(*Good-naturedly*)

I wanted to, Christopherson, but the Chinese wouldn't let me. They said I ought to come back and convert Americans. And, by God, I think I'll start with you first one. You need reformin' worse than anyone I know of. And speakin' of that subject— how is she, and whereabouts and all that? I'm just interested in gettin' a bit of news.

CHRIS

Anna don't vant see you no more.

MAT

I didn't say she did. I'm just askin' how is she, that's all.

CHRIS

(*Suddenly*)

She's married.

MAT

(*Pause*)

You don't tell me. Well, I wish her well. And him, too, who-ever he is. So let's go somewheres and have a drink to the happy couple. My treat!

CHRIS

Ay don't vant no drink.

MAT

I'm no grudge-holder. I hope you ain't.

CHRIS

Ay don't hold grudge. Yust so long you leave my Anna alone.

MAT

Can I make it any plainer, man? Them days is over—dead.

CHRIS

Ay ain't goin' lose her.

MAT

If she's married, you've lost her already.
(HENRY *enters carrying a bushel basket full of potatoes on his hip.*)

HENRY

Howdy, Chris? We was wonderin' whether you'd be here.

130

CHRIS

(*Alarmed*)

Yeah. But Ay got to go. Henry, Ay got to go have a drink friend here. (*Quickly grabs* MAT *and starts to pull him away*) Ve go, Mat, ve go out dis vay.

HENRY

(*As they go*)

Anna'll be sorry to miss you.
  (MAT *walks a couple of steps and then stops.*)

MAT

(*To* HENRY)

Anna!

HENRY

Yeah. She's off by the wagon.

CHRIS

Come on, ve get drink.

MAT

(*To* CHRIS)

You mean this fellow is her—

HENRY

(*Calling*)

Anna—your father's here.

CHRIS

Some other time ve see her.

MAT

There ain't no other time. I'm gonna be in port but one day.
(ANNA, *wearing coarse old farm clothes, enters carrying a bushel basket full of potatoes. At first she notices only her father.*)

CHRIS

Anna, you come too early—

ANNA

Hello, Father, I—(*Sees* MAT. *She stops*) Oh. (*Puts down the basket*) Imagine—

MAT

I've been away.

CHRIS

Vant me to help you vid your basket, Anna?
(*He lifts one end of the basket in an effort to lead her off.* HENRY *grabs the other end, foiling him.*)

HENRY

Yes, siree. We'll take them. You stay here, Anna, and visit with your friend.

CHRIS

(*Surprised*)

Vat?

HENRY

Keep hold of that now, Chris. Easy does it.
(HENRY *and* CHRIS *go out carrying the basket.*)

MAT

Didn't take you long to get married. Did it?

ANNA

What?

MAT

(*Laughing*)

Don't that beat hell? Here I am feelin' so cocky 'cause I got over you, and then when I find how easy you got over me I don't like it. Sure—I heard the news. Your father told me. We're only in port a few hours. Headed for Norfolk. So I thought I'd like to find out if you was still around, or where you was at, or somethin'.

ANNA

Well, I'm still here.

MAT

And lookin' fine, too.

ANNA

(*A little defiant—embarrassed*)

I don't go in for the looks much these days.

MAT

Sure you look different, but you look—I don't know—like you was all right.

ANNA

(*Defiantly*)

I am. (*Collecting herself*) How are *you*?

MAT

You know how it is. I'm all right. Pulled a tooth yesterday.

ANNA

Some people are sayin' maybe you shouldn't let them pull teeth. You should fix them instead.

MAT

Feller tied a string to it, and boom.

ANNA

Ugh!

MAT

No—felt good. I mean to be rid of it. No high price charge for the job, neither. Red Saunders. That's the guy's name. He pulls all the teeth. He likes it.

ANNA

Maybe he should of been a dentist.

MAT

(*Looking down*)

Anna—it's always been botherin' me, some of the things I said to you.

ANNA

It's all over—it don't matter. I'm all over it.

MAT

Sittin' here so easy and quiet. Like we was two different people almost.

134

ANNA

Gee! Ain't we different!

MAT

I don't know.

ANNA

After you go through somethin' like that, you gotta be.
(CHRIS *enters, crosses toward them but is stopped by* SMITH, *who comes out of the office.*)

SMITH

Christopherson. Just the man I want.
(SMITH *leads* CHRIS *into the office.* HENRY *enters.*)

HENRY

Anna, you goin' back on the ferry with me?

ANNA

Yes, Henry. I'll make it.

HENRY

Good-bye, mister.
(*He exits.*)

MAT

What time's your ferry?

ANNA

Not yet. About twenty minutes. Listen, Mat, my father, you know how he is?

MAT

Yeah, I know how he is, but what about it?

ANNA

Well, it don't matter a jot one way or the other, but I ain't married.

MAT

No? What's this carryin' bushel baskets and all that stuff?

ANNA

I'm workin' on a farm in Staten Island.

MAT

You're a farmer?

ANNA

Ain't that a scream?

MAT

You always used to hate that most of anythin'.

ANNA

Maybe I still do.

MAT

Yeah?

ANNA

But I've been doin' it for a year, now. That shows somethin', don't it?

MAT

Liftin' spuds? Man's work. Shows what?

ANNA

Shows I ain't good for nothin'.
> (CHRIS *enters from the office.*)

CHRIS

Anna, Ay tank you have nice long talk, now . . .

ANNA

> (*To* MAT)

Anyhow, it makes me feel good.

CHRIS

You don't vant keep Henry vaiting.

ANNA

Well, good-bye.

MAT

Good-bye.
> (*They pause. Streetwalkers and men enter.*)

MOLL

. . . For the Seaman's Home.

VIOLET

Where at?

PEARL

Right here. Oh, sure, we don't want to miss that.

MAT

Say, Anna. I don't feel right about somethin' . . . I don't know what. Ain't there no ferry in an hour or so? I'll take you out—get somethin' to eat.

ANNA

You sure you don't want to do somethin' else? Go have yourself a good time or somethin'?

CHRIS

You start valking now, you yust have time.

MAT

Hey, can we have a private conversation, please? (*To* ANNA) Will you, Anna?

ANNA

I'd have to tell Henry.

MAT

Sure, go ahead—tell him and then meet me later.

CHRIS

Ay say no. You can't go out vid sailor fella—you go vid society peoples from Staten Island.

138

ANNA

You sure got a clear picture (*The sound of a drum is heard offstage*) of everythin' about me. (*She looks in the direction of the sound*) Here comes a friend of yours. (*She exits.*)

CHRIS

Listen, sailor fella, ay tell you vun ting.

MAT

All right, what?

CHRIS

Since you gone avay, Ay don't heard Anna not vunce speak your name.

MAT

Okey doke, squarehead. Now, I'll tell you somethin'. I'm goin' away in a few hours, and you ain't gonna heard it spoke again for another year—so quit fussin'.

IVY

Gather 'round, everybody, gather 'round.
    (*The drum becomes louder.*)

MAT

For the love of Mike!
    (*Four proper women enter; one is carrying a big base drum and all are in Seamen's Home uniforms.* MARTHY *follows, similarly dressed. She sees* MAT, *starts for him, but is rebuked.*)

MARTHY

Hey, Mat.

CAPTAIN OF THE LADIES
(*Snapping her fingers*)

Marthy.

(MARTHY *returns to her place*.)

(MARTHY *and* GIRLS *sing*)

You are W-E-L-C-O-M-E at the Seamen's Home.

(MARTHY, *as* GIRLS *hum*)
You hear W-E-L-C-O-M-E ringin' 'cross the foam.

(MARTHY *and* GIRLS)
We're an institution that deserves your contribution
'Cause you're always welcome at the Seamen's

(MARTHY, *as* GIRLS *hum*)
H-O-M-E, Home.

(MARTHY *and* GIRLS)
We give you chess and checkers,
And real companionship.
Gospel singin' Friday night.

(MARTHY)
Home cooked navy beans,
Last year's magazines,

(MARTHY *and* GIRLS)
Makin' all your evenin's bright.

(ALL)
You'll give us chess and checkers,
And real companionship.

Gospel singin' Friday night.
Home cooked navy beans,
Last year's magazines,
Makin' all our evenin's bright.

(POOR SOUL)
I'd make a contribution, but what more can I say?
Than I have thirteen mouths to feed
And one more on the way.

(CAPTAIN)
Well, if you need assistance, we'll feed the little scamps.

(MARTHY)
And try to int'rest daddy in hobby craft or stamps.

(ALL)
We'll give him chess and checkers,
And real championship,

(ALL GIRLS)
Gospel singin' Friday night.

(ALL MEN)
Gospel singin' Friday night.

(ALL)
Home cooked navy beans,
Last year's magazines,
Makin' all his evenin's bright.

(MARTHY *and* GIRLS)
Lots of wholesome recreation,
Rockin' chairs for contemplation.

For your soul's regeneration.
Dumpty, dumpity dum.

(MARTHY)
Down with demon rum.

(ALL)
You give us chess and checkers,
And real companionship,
Gospel singin' Friday night.

(MARTHY *and* GIRLS)
A Christmas chicken pick
An Easter pic-i-nic.

(ALL)
Makin' all our holidays bright.

(ANOTHER SOUL)
This dollar's for my uncle who died this Thursday past.

(MARTHY)
Well, bring him over anyway, we'll give it to him fast.

(ALL)
We'll give him chess and checkers,
And real companionship,
Gospel singin' Friday night.
Christmas chicken pick— Easter pic-i-nic.
Makin' all his holidays
Chess and checkers
Chess and checkers
Home cooked navy beans and last year's magazines
Makin' all our evenin's
Chess and checkers—real companionship.

MRS. SMITH

Come on now, everybody, dig down for a good cause.

MRS. DOWLING

You always got plenty for the saloon, so dig down for the poor homeless seamen.

MRS. HAMMACHER

Put your hands in your pockets and see if you haven't a thin dime to help us out.

IVY

Where you goin' in your old age? The Seamen's Home.

LARRY

Marthy, one for old times.
(MARTHY *passes the hat.*)

MARTHY

Come on, Dutchy, shell out and set a good example.

CHRIS

Marthy, I got to talk vit you.

MARTHY

Just the price of a beer for a worthy cause—that's all I ask.

CHRIS

Dat fella's back—dat Mat Burke.

MARTHY

I know, I know. Still good-lookin', ain't he?

BASE DRUMMER

Seaman Owen, Spring Street is next.

MARTHY

Aye, aye. I'll follow you. First I gotta have a little talk with this poor wanderer.
(*The proper women exit.*)

CHRIS

Marthy, vat's he up to?
(*One of the trollops tries unsuccessfully to make contact with* MAT.)

MARTHY

Right now he's flaggin' a fast freight . . . No. I'm wrong.

CHRIS

Ay don't know vat to do. Anna say she come back here and talk to him some more. Marthy. How'm Ay find out vat she tankin'?

MARTHY

When she comes in, you'll know. If she's still got on them Staten Island potato sacks . . .

CHRIS

Look—she's comin'.

MARTHY

Well, look her up and down and draw your own conclusions.
> (ANNA *enters. She no longer wears the farm dress but has
> changed into something special.*)

(MAT *sings*)
Look at 'er, look at 'er,
Excuse me while I look at 'er,
And melt just like I'm butter in the sun.

ANNA

I hurried—as fast as I could.

MAT

A mermaid.

ANNA

What?

MAT

Remember that first time I seen you?

ANNA

That's a long time ago, Mat.

MAT

Yeah, I know, but you're still here.

ANNA

You're still here, too. For a couple of hours, anyway.

MAT

There's ships run both ways. I can come back.
(*She comes close to him.*)

ANNA

Please come back.

MARTHY

You'll always be welcome at the Seamen's Home.
(MAT *gives* ANNA *the ring from his ear and sings*)
But now I realize
The reason I have eyes.
(*He picks her up in his arms.*)

ANNA

Mat!
(MAT *continues singing*)
Is just to look at 'er, look at 'er, look at 'er.

CURTAIN